Meet the Musicians

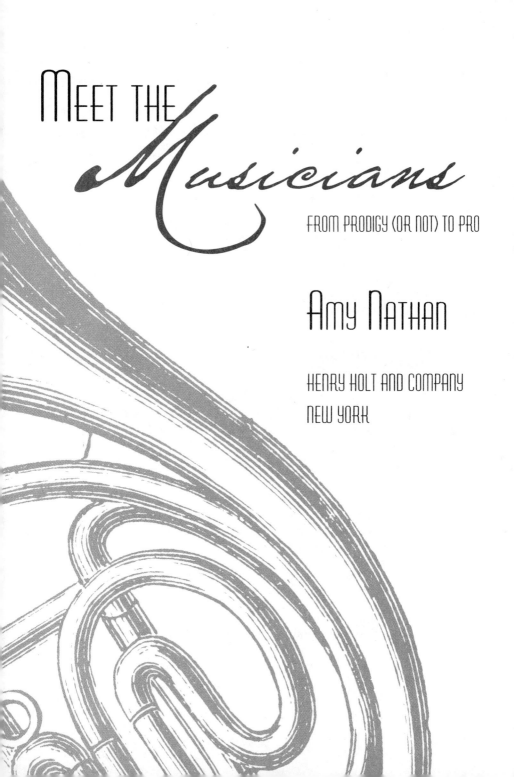

MEET THE
Musicians

FROM PRODIGY (OR NOT) TO PRO

AMY NATHAN

HENRY HOLT AND COMPANY
NEW YORK

Photo Credits

All photos of the musicians as kids appear courtesy of the individual musicians. Front cover (top, far left and far right), back cover, ii (top three and bottom), vii (bottom), 23, 52, 63, 70, 81, 96, 97, 113, 121, 131, 137, 138, 142: © 2004 or 2005 Michael DiVito; front cover (top, second from left) © Susan Johann; vi (top), 34: © 1999 Chris Lee; vi (bottom), 11, 41, 42: © 2004 or 2005 Chris Lee; 2: © 2003 Leo Sorel; 31: © Lisa Kohler; 53: © 2001 David Morris, courtesy of Curtis Institute of Music; 12: © Yeui Park, courtesy of JCC Thurnauer School of Music of Tenafly, New Jersey; 107: © 2005 Amy Nathan; 87: courtesy Judith LeClair

Henry Holt and Company, LLC
Publishers since 1866
175 Fifth Avenue
New York, New York 10010
www.henryholtchildrensbooks.com

Henry Holt® is a registered trademark of Henry Holt and Company, LLC.
Text copyright © 2006 by Amy Nathan
All rights reserved.
Distributed in Canada by H. B. Fenn and Company Ltd.

Library of Congress Cataloging-in-Publication Data
Nathan, Amy.
Meet the musicians: from prodigy (or not) to pro / Amy Nathan.—
1st ed.
p.   cm.
Includes index.
Summary: Musicians from many different sections of the New York
Philharmonic describe how they became involved in music as kids.
Includes advice and practice tips for kids.
ISBN-13: 978-0-8050-7743-8 / ISBN-10: 0-8050-7743-X
1. Musicians—Biography—Juvenile literature.   I. Title.
ML3929.N37 2006   780.92'273—dc22   2005026508

First Edition—2006
Printed in the United States of America on acid-free paper. ∞
10 9 8 7 6 5 4 3 2 1
A portion of the proceeds from this book will go toward promoting
music education.

FOR CARL, ERIC, AND NOAH

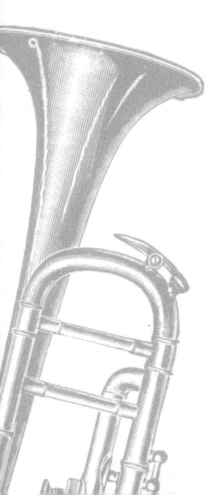

MEET THE *Musicians*

New York Philharmonic musicians Carter Brey, with his cello, and
Cynthia Phelps, with her viola, all dressed up for a performance.

Introduction

Catching the Beat

"When I'm on stage, I think I'm the luckiest person in the world, having such a good time doing what I love to do," says Cynthia Phelps. She's a musician and a member of the New York Philharmonic, one of the best orchestras in the world. So is Carter Brey, the musician standing next to her in the photo on the opposite page. They're holding the instruments they play. She plays viola, a string instrument that's like a violin, only a little bigger. He plays an even larger string instrument, a cello.

They're both in their best concert clothes, ready to play music for the hundreds of people who will be in the audience at the concert hall where the orchestra performs in New York City. Sometimes, millions of people all across the country can also listen to the orchestra's concerts. That's because several times a year, New York Philharmonic concerts are broadcast live on radio and TV stations around the country, and on the Internet, too.

The path that Cynthia and Carter took to end up in this orchestra started when they were kids. In this book, you'll meet Carter and Cynthia as kids. You'll also meet thirteen other "kids" who grew up to be Philharmonic musicians. They tell how they got started in music. You might be surprised to find out that many were definitely *not* super at music right from the start. Several even took quite a while to discover which type of musical instrument they wanted to play.

Another surprise: Some of these musicians didn't like to practice as children and didn't spend much time doing it at first. They were busy with so many other things they liked to do. However, there came a time when something magical clicked between them and their instruments. Sometimes it was the beauty of a special piece of music that did the trick. Others were inspired by a terrific teacher or a great group of kids. Practicing no longer seemed like a chore. Instead, it was something they *wanted* to do so they could make wonderful music. Even so, all those other experiences they enjoyed when they were young—swimming, dancing, reading, sailing, skating, drawing, hiking, horseback riding—played a part in helping them become the great musicians they are today.

In the following pages, these musicians also share practice strategies that helped them to master their instruments. Plus, they tell what to do on days when you absolutely don't want to practice. After all, they had days like that. In addition, they fill you in on the good and bad points of their instruments, and explain what they love about music. Cynthia notes, "Ever since I was a kid, I've loved to perform. It's like giving a gift of something beautiful to help other people feel good."

Although the musicians in this book play with the New York Philharmonic, their experiences are similar to those of performers in other orchestras. The resources at the end of the book lists ways to find out about other orchestras.

As a kid, Carter Brey loved playing outdoors.

CARTER BREY
Cello

Age when he started cello: 12 (started violin at 9)
Pet he had as a kid: Dog named Randolph
Pets he has now: Cats named Ginger and Thomas
Favorite books as a kid: Horatio Hornblower books by C. S. Forester
Other activities as a kid: Running, sailing, swimming, taking flying lessons
Other activities now: Running, sailing, playing with his kids
Grew up in: Westchester County, New York
Education: Peabody Institute; Yale University
Before the Philharmonic: Cleveland Orchestra; freelance soloist
Joined New York Philharmonic: 1996 as Principal Cello
Music he listens to now when relaxing: Classical, jazz, pop, country

One day when Carter Brey was five years old, he was sick in bed with a bad cold. To cheer him up, his dad put on a new recording he had just bought. Carter's dad loved music. He wasn't a professional musician, but he liked to play the piano, just for fun.

The recording had a piece on it that had been written especially for kids: *The Young Person's Guide to the Orchestra* by British composer Benjamin

INSIDE SCOOP: CELLO

GOOD POINTS: "A cello's low, deep sound is easy on the ears. You don't have to worry about neighbors complaining when you practice because it's not very loud—an advantage over the trumpet," says Carter Brey.

BAD POINTS: "A cello's soft sound makes it difficult to be heard in a large hall," he says. "A cello is also big and hard to travel with," adds Hai-Ye Ni, another cellist you'll meet in this book. "I have to buy a ticket for my cello on airplanes. It sits in the seat next to me."

Britten. It's a lively piece in which different instruments take turns being the main ones you hear. When it's the violins' turn to shine, they burst in with a fast-paced, rollicking tune. Their dazzling sound whizzes by, zooming up high and then sliding down low. Next come other string instruments: violas, cellos, and basses.

"I completely fell in love with the sound of those string instruments," Carter remembers. He decided he wanted to play a string instrument someday.

However, when he had his first chance to do so, things didn't work out right away. He was nine years old and in fourth grade. That's when kids at his elementary school could choose an instrument to play. He chose violin and joined a class with other beginners. Some beginners do well on violin right from the start. Not Carter. Instead of sounding like the wonderful violins on that recording he loved, for a long time he sounded very squeaky and scratchy. He was kind of discouraged. But he didn't give up.

"AN UPHILL BATTLE"

"Violin is hard when you first start," Carter says. It wasn't like his dad's piano. With a piano, anyone can make a pretty good sound just by pressing a key. It's not so easy to make a good sound on a violin or other string instrument. You have to press on the strings with the fingers of one hand in exactly the right way— not too hard and not too soft. With your other hand, you have to hold a stick called a bow and get the hang of sliding it across the strings to make a sound.

"It was an uphill battle for me," says Carter. "I wasn't getting anywhere on that squeaky little thing." He kept at it all through elementary school, but he didn't practice often and didn't make much progress. When he moved on to junior high, he decided it was time for a change. He thought he might make nicer noises on something with a lower sound, such as a cello. So at age twelve, he asked the junior high music teacher if he could switch instruments.

Success at last! "I made a much better sound on the cello," Carter says. "I enjoyed it more than violin." But music still wasn't a big deal to him yet. There were so many other things he liked to do. He ran on the school's track team. He liked to go sailing with his dad and swimming with his friends. He spent a lot of time exploring in the woods near his house with his dog, Randolph. He and a friend even took flying lessons at a nearby airport.

"I continued with group cello lessons in school, using one of the school's cellos. I played in the school orchestra, just muddling along," he says. "But I didn't practice much. My parents didn't bug me to practice, either. Cello was just a mild interest—*until* I was fifteen. Then it became a passion."

"COULDN'T LIVE WITHOUT MUSIC"

What turned him around? "I discovered how great music for cello could be," he recalls. He was in high school by then. The school's music teacher divided the students into groups and had them play chamber music, pieces that are written for small numbers of players. "The pieces were way too hard for us," Carter says. But he loved the challenge of trying to master such great works.

"There was one piece we played that made me realize I couldn't live without music in my life." That was the beautiful String Quintet in C Major by Austrian composer Franz Schubert. It's written for five instruments: two cellos, two violins, and a viola. After he started learning to play this quintet in school,

---

PRACTICE TIP

SMALL CHUNKS: "Break down a piece you're learning into small goals," says Carter Brey. "For example, decide to learn just one page today. Or take one phrase and see how perfect you can make it today. Then go on to the next page or phrase tomorrow. If you break down a task into small parts like that, it's a much easier burden to bear. You'll make more progress, too."

he bought a recording of it. "It was thrilling to come home and put that record on my little portable record player and hear the incredible sound of that piece. It was a mind-blowing experience. I decided that I was going to become a musician."

That was a big decision for a teenager who hadn't been practicing much, knew little about music, and wasn't even very good on his instru-ment. "I knew I could

Carter performs with the New York Philharmonic.

do it. Don't ask me how. I just knew."

Through friends, he found a private cello teacher to study with outside of school. He had his first lesson with her right after his sixteenth birthday. "I had to start over from the beginning," he says. "It didn't dis-courage me. I was ready to make the commitment to getting good on the instrument. She taught me how to practice. She started me on a steady diet of scales and études [technical exercises]. I didn't find it boring. I

Carter sometimes teaches workshops, giving helpful tips to young cellists, as he's doing here.

saw it was helping. I couldn't wait to get home and work on this stuff."

"YOU STILL CAN"

"People are amazed that I didn't start private cello lessons until I was sixteen," he says. Many musicians (including ones you'll meet in this book) start private lessons when they're much younger. "But sixteen is young enough that if you have a very strong desire to excel, you still can," Carter explains. "With a five-year-old, if the child isn't really interested, private lessons aren't going to have much effect. Yes, I was sixteen, but I was passionate and self-motivated. It was *my* decision."

He started practicing every day. "I would get up early and practice before school. I practiced during school, too, whenever I had a study hall period," he recalls. After school, he had a job cleaning up at a music store. Then he would come home, do his homework, and practice cello some more. His parents saw how serious he had become and bought him his own instrument.

To make room for all this extra practicing, he stopped his flying lessons. He dropped out of the track team, too. But he kept running on his own for fun, and he kept sailing. Running, sailing, and flying taught him things that wound up helping him with music. "Getting through a difficult cello performance takes concentration and pacing yourself, just like running a marathon," he explains. "Sailing is about balance and making judgments, a combination of art and science. So is flying. So is music."

THE PATH TO THE PHILHARMONIC

When Carter was seventeen, it was time to think about college. He wanted to go to a conservatory, a special school just for music. His parents weren't sure that was wise. They weren't musicians. They didn't know if he

CONCERT WATCH

Next time you're at an orchestra concert, watch what cellists do with the endpin, the metal spike that sticks out of the bottom of a cello. Many cellists stick the endpin into a little cup at the end of a belt-like holder that attaches to the leg of their chair to keep the cello from slipping while they play. Carter Brey does that when performing in private homes or in places with stone floors. But at the Philharmonic's concert hall in New York City, he just jams the endpin right into the stage's wooden floor. "The orchestra managers beg us not to, but we do it anyway," he says. "It's nice to be able to jam the point into the floor and make the tiny adjustments in angle this allows you." However, until you become principal cellist in an orchestra like the Philharmonic, it's probably wise to keep using that belt-like holder.

was good enough to make it in the world of music. "When I won a scholarship to go to a major music conservatory, they realized I knew what I was doing," says Carter.

After studying cello at this conservatory—the Peabody Institute in Baltimore, Maryland—he did more cello studies at Yale University in New Haven, Connecticut. Then he landed a job as a cellist with the Cleveland Orchestra in Ohio. Two years later, he won a prize in an important international cello competition. That gave him the courage to quit the Cleveland job and set out on his own as a soloist, someone who plays as a special guest artist with different orchestras. For fourteen years he was a soloist with some of the most famous orchestras in the world.

He was always traveling to different cities to play in concerts. That was fun at first. But after he married and had kids, he didn't want to be away from his family so much. Luckily, a cello job opened up at the New York Philharmonic. He tried out for it and in 1996 won the job of being the orchestra's principal cello. That means he's the leader of the cello section.

He still plays as a soloist now and then, sometimes with the Philharmonic or with other orchestras. The Philharmonic gives him time off to do this. But for most of the year he is with his wife and kids in New York City, performing with the Philharmonic. "I still practice every day," he says, "and I still love the cello's sound."

Sheryl Staples playing violin on the
Lawrence Welk Show *on TV, with her sister and mom*
at the piano.

SHERYL STAPLES
Violin

Age when she started violin: 5
Pet she had as a kid: Dog named Patches
Favorite books as a kid: The Chronicles of Narnia by C. S. Lewis, and books by Judy Blume
Other activities as a kid: Gymnastics, roller skating, Brownies, water skiing, motorboat trips with her family
Other activities now: Gardening, playing with her kids
Grew up in: Los Angeles, California
Education: University of Southern California
Before the Philharmonic: Santa Barbara Chamber Orchestra; Pacific Symphony; Cleveland Orchestra
Joined New York Philharmonic: 1998 as Principal Associate Concertmaster
Teaches at: The Juilliard School
Music she listens to now when relaxing: Classical

A dog named Patches made practicing violin tricky for Sheryl Staples. "He would howl when I started practicing," she says. Patches joined the family when Sheryl was about ten. By then she had been playing violin for five years. Her mom recalls that Sheryl sounded great right from the start. Sheryl could tell if a note she played was a little out of tune, a little sour. If it

INSIDE SCOOP: VIOLIN

GOOD POINTS: "You can make the most beautiful, human-like sound on a violin. It can really sing," explains Sheryl Staples. "The range of colors and tones is endless. You can hold a tone for a very long time, much longer than wind or brass players, who eventually have to stop and take a breath. In an orchestra, violins play almost constantly, creating a wonderful blanket of sound." Another plus: Violins are light and easy to carry.

BAD POINTS: "Producing a beautiful sound on a string instrument is a challenge," she adds. "There are no markers on the strings to show where to put your fingers. You have to train your fingers to go down in exactly the right places."

was, she knew how to fix it by changing where she put her fingers on the strings. Many beginners can't easily do that at first.

But beautiful playing didn't matter to Patches. "There was something about the sound of a violin that bothered him," Sheryl explains. "If he was outside the window where I was practicing, he would howl like a wolf. I had to practice on the other side of the house from him. I liked playing violin as a child, but I can't say I liked practicing." That wasn't just because she had to switch rooms to keep her dog happy. "When I was ten, I was supposed to practice thirty minutes a day in order to get my allowance. Some days I practiced that much, but not every day. I wasn't that serious about it then."

Violin was just a hobby to Sheryl. But before long, she met up with some kids who inspired her to turn music into much more than a hobby.

"KIND OF EXCITING"

Sheryl started violin almost by chance. Her parents happened to have an old kid-size violin stashed away in the closet. It had belonged to Sheryl's aunt when she was a little girl. Sheryl's parents had begun to realize that their daughter really liked music. She was always singing songs. So when Sheryl was five years old, her dad pulled the tiny violin out of the closet and showed it to her. "It looked kind of exciting," Sheryl remembers. Soon she was taking lessons on that little violin from a teacher who lived near their home in Los Angeles.

"I did well for a few months," says Sheryl. "Then I quit!" Her teacher wanted Sheryl to learn how to read music, and she just couldn't get it. Luckily, her mom found a new violin teacher who used a different way of teaching—the Suzuki method. Suzuki teachers don't have kids read music at first. "You start playing by ear, imitating what the teacher plays," Sheryl explains. "The Suzuki method saved me." She made good progress. Before long, she was not only playing well, she was reading music, too.

Unfortunately, there weren't good music programs in the first schools she attended. She didn't have the fun of playing in an elementary or middle school orchestra. "I performed a solo at our sixth-grade graduation, but mostly I was taking private lessons and playing pieces by myself," she says. Even so, she thinks it's "good to do something like music at an early age. It gives you a feeling of self-confidence."

She was also doing some other confidence-boosting activities, such as being in a Scout troop and taking gymnastics classes. "I loved gymnastics, especially tumbling," says Sheryl. She liked to water ski and roller skate, too. She and her sister, Deborah, liked to make up skating routines to songs from the movie *Grease*. They would put on shows for visiting relatives. They also performed on TV, not doing skating routines, but playing music. Her father played trombone in a band on a weekly TV show. At Christmas, families of band members had a chance to perform on the show. Sheryl and her sister did this a few times, with Sheryl playing violin and her sister playing piano.

"TOTALLY CHANGED MY LIFE"

By the time Sheryl was thirteen, she had a new private violin teacher who was helping her learn a better way to hold and play the violin. He also helped her win a scholarship to a private high school that specialized in the arts. It had

---

PRACTICE TIP

JUST LIKE SPORTS: "Playing a musical instrument is like playing a sport," says Sheryl Staples. "Your muscles have to stay in shape to play well in both sports and music." Regular practice helps, whether you're learning to throw a curve ball or play a tricky passage on violin. "If you spend just a few minutes on it every day, even if you don't feel like you're getting anywhere, it will be a little easier the next day. Each day you'll get a little better until finally you can do it. Kids get frustrated when they can't do things right away. If you keep at it, you can achieve incredible things."

an excellent music program. "That school totally changed my life," she says.

"Suddenly I was around kids who were serious about music," Sheryl explains. "I hadn't known many kids like that before. I wasn't the best one at the school, either. The school attracted talented kids from all over the Los Angeles area. I wanted to play as well as these other kids. So I started taking more interest in practicing."

At this school, she finally had a chance to play in a school orchestra. She loved it. "We played really difficult pieces. The conductor was very demanding. It was exciting. I loved the challenge. When we played concerts, people couldn't believe it was a bunch of kids." In the summers during high school she wanted to keep working on her violin skills, and so she went to special music camps that were just for string players.

"LISTENING ALL THE TIME"

In addition to improving as a violinist, Sheryl learned something else: how to listen. She picked this up partly from a boy who went to her high school. Sheryl and the boy both lived far from the school and carpooled there each day. "He had tons of cassette tapes of classical music that we listened to on the long drive to school. He knew so much about the music. I didn't know anything. We didn't have many records at home. I hadn't heard much classical music before. I listened keenly to his recordings and his comments. It was a huge education for me. I started going to music stores and convinced my parents that I needed to buy recordings. Soon I was listening all the time—in the car and at home. Listening is so important. You not only learn about the music, you also hear what professional musicians sound like on your instrument. Once you get that sound in your ear, that's the first step to being able to produce such a sound yourself."

Her private teacher also stressed the importance of listening. He took Sheryl to concerts and asked what she thought about what she heard. "At first, I didn't know what to say. Everything sounded good," says Sheryl. Her teacher had her focus on details, such as what she thought of the violinists' tone, how in tune they were, how they handled themselves on stage. "Live concerts are so different from recordings. You can watch the musicians, see their technique, learn from them." She also learned to listen carefully to her fellow students when they played music at school. And she learned to listen carefully to her own playing, to hear both what was good about it and what could be better.

THE PATH TO THE PHILHARMONIC

After high school, she took a year off to spend time practicing and playing chamber music. She also joined an orchestra of college-age musicians. Then she studied music at the University of Southern California. While there and for a few years after graduating, she played lots of chamber music and performed with

The New York Philharmonic gives several concerts for kids each year. Often before these concerts, or right afterward, orchestra members come into the lobby to meet audience members, as Sheryl is doing in these two photos.

several local orchestras, both as a soloist and a concert-master. The Cleveland Orchestra invited her to try out to be its associate concertmaster. She won the job.

CONCERT WATCH

After an orchestra finishes playing a piece, keep your eye on the concertmaster (who sits at the head of the violin section). The conductor will often shake hands with some orchestra members, usually starting with the concertmaster. If a soloist performs with the orchestra, he or she will usually shake the concertmaster's hand, too. "They can't shake everyone's hand on stage," notes Sheryl Staples. "So they shake hands with the concertmaster, who acts as the representative for all the musicians."

Three years later, in 1998, she won another job, becoming the New York Philharmonic's principal associate concertmaster.

A concertmaster is the head of an orchestra's violin section and also the official leader of all the orchestra's other musicians. At the start of a concert, after all the other musicians are on stage, the concertmaster walks on stage as the audience applauds. Then the concertmaster has the musicians "tune up." They play the same note to be sure they're all playing that note alike—not too high and not too low. Most orchestras give so many concerts that sometimes musicians are able to take a break and not play in every concert. When the regular concertmaster isn't there, an associate concertmaster, like Sheryl, takes over the role.

Sheryl doesn't perform only in the Philharmonic. She also plays chamber music and sometimes is a soloist with other orchestras. In addition, she teaches a class at the Juilliard School in New York City. Sheryl also finds time to practice every day, but she no longer has to worry about a howling dog. Her family doesn't have a dog now. However, her two young children can get cranky if she practices when they feel she should be playing with them. Sheryl usually practices late at night, after they're asleep, noting, "Luckily, my practicing doesn't wake them up."

*Chris Lamb with a go-cart he built
himself for coasting down
a hill near his house.*

CHRISTOPHER LAMB
Percussion

Age when he started drums: 7 (started piano in junior high)
Pets he had as a kid: A rat named Ricky-the-Rat-a-Tat-Tat, and a snake
Favorite books as kid: Civil War and World War II books
Other activities as a kid: Baseball, basketball, biking, swimming, an after-school job (paper route)
Other activities now: Mountain biking; swimming; basketball; playing with his kids; collecting whistles, clickers, drums, and other instruments from around the world
Grew up in: Flint, Michigan
Education: Eastman School of Music
Before the Philharmonic: Buffalo Philharmonic; Metropolitan Opera Orchestra
Joined New York Philharmonic: 1985 as Principal Percussion
Teaches at: Manhattan School of Music
Music he listens to now when relaxing: Jazz or Latin

"We bought Chris a drum when he was seven in order to save the furniture," says Christopher Lamb's mom. "He was always tapping on everything with his fingers." His dad adds, "The coffee table was so wobbly from his hitting it that it was a wonder it could still stand. But he wasn't just making noise. He could make different sounds by hitting it differently."

INSIDE SCOOP: PERCUSSION

<u>GOOD POINTS:</u> "The best thing is the variety," says Chris Lamb. "There are hundreds of percussion instruments. It never gets dull. I like the energy, the feeling that something is really happening. I'll be playing and sweating like crazy, but I love it."

<u>BAD POINTS:</u> "There's a lot of gear, a lot of instruments to learn," he points out. "When you're a kid setting up your stuff at a concert, some parent always walks by and says, 'Don't you wish you played piccolo?'"

His parents weren't musicians and knew nothing about drums. After buying a used drum, they arranged for Chris to take lessons from a high school senior who was an excellent drummer. "We asked the high school boy to be sure Chris learned how to read music," his mom explains. "We figured when Chris found out that it wasn't just banging, that you had to count, he'd lose interest. It didn't work out that way. It turned out just the opposite."

Chris loved the drum. "The tapping had focus now," Chris says. "I was a very active kid. I always had to be doing something. This was a way to use that energy for a purpose." He was also happy to learn that he wasn't the only person who liked to tap out rhythms on things. Here was a teenager who did it, too. The high schooler taught Chris basic drumming techniques. "He gave me assignments, and I did them," says Chris.

"I was really interested in playing *and* practicing. Nobody ever had to bug me to practice." When that teenager graduated from high school, Chris moved on to other teachers. They soon had Chris tapping on more things than drums—or coffee tables.

"JUST DOING WHAT I DID"

Chris took lessons from his elementary school's music teacher next and then studied with the owner of a local drum shop. His school didn't have a band, but in fourth grade he was asked to play a drum solo at a school assembly. "That was the first time I performed in public," he says. The audience loved his performance. "I was surprised," he says. He hadn't realized there was anything special about his drumming. "I was up there just doing what I did."

However, things didn't go so well at the start of junior high school. Chris received a C in music for the first marking period in seventh grade. That year, he was in a school band for the first time, in the percussion section. He hadn't known how many percussion instruments there were besides drums. He had to take tests on many of them, including playing bells and xylophone. He wasn't practicing much on anything but drums and did poorly on some tests. Even so, the teacher believed in this young drummer. The teacher encouraged him and even visited Chris's dad at work to say that the boy had talent and could do so much more. Those comments changed Chris. "I began to apply myself," he says. "By the end of the year, the teacher gave me a scholarship to go to a music camp over the summer."

"SOMETHING HAD TO GIVE"

Music camp opened up a new world to Chris. For the first time, he had a chance to play in an orchestra. He heard classical music, something he hadn't heard at home. Also, he was with kids who were as excited about percussion as he was. However, they were better than Chris on some instruments. He came home determined to improve. He began taking piano lessons in addition to drum lessons. Piano helps with other percussion instruments, such as xylophone, marimba, and vibraphone. To play these, you use a mallet to strike wooden or metal bars that are laid out very much like a piano's keyboard. Before long, Chris was studying with a marimba and vibraphone teacher at a local music school. The next summer, he went back to music camp and won an award.

Chris was also busy playing on basketball and baseball teams during junior high. In the summer, he went swimming at a lake. In his free time, he'd go biking or shoot hoops with neighborhood kids and his five brothers

PRACTICE TIP

START SLOW: "Practice from slow to fast," suggests Chris Lamb. "People always want to play fast. But when you practice, start slow so you're in control of each note. Then you can get a little faster, bit by bit." This is good advice for any instrument, but it's especially important in practicing basic drum strokes. "Start slow, controlling it, then go faster and faster until you get to the point of just letting it go. That will make you a better player."

and sisters. He also had an after-school job delivering newspapers. "By the time I was in ninth grade, it was clear that if I was going to take all those music lessons, something had to give. I gave up team sports," he says. "Instead, I did things I could do by myself, like swimming, biking, or running."

"PASSIONATE ABOUT PLAYING"

His parents bought him a drum set but couldn't afford many other instruments, and so Chris had to be resourceful. "The guy at the drum shop

Here's Chris with some of his percussion instruments. Behind him are (from right to left) a big bass drum, a gong, chimes, and a snare drum. In front of Chris is a xylophone, and sitting on top of it is a shekere, an African instrument made from a gourd covered in a mesh with beads on it that make a sound when you shake the shekere.

had instruments in his back room that he let me play," Chris says. "At the local music school, I had permission to practice on their instruments. The janitor would let me in. I practiced on the marimba at my high school. Over summer vacation, I was able to bring home some of the school's instruments. I figured out ways to do it. I was passionate about playing."

In his first years of high school, Chris played in the school orchestra, concert band, jazz band, marching band, and drum and bugle corps. In his last two years, he wasn't in any school groups because he was busy playing in a youth orchestra on weekends in Ann Arbor, Michigan, more than an hour's drive away. Sometimes he played in his hometown orchestra, the Flint Symphony, if it needed extra percussionists. In addition, he was taking private lessons in Detroit, also about an hour away. "I moved through a lot of teachers," he says. There were so many instruments to learn: drums, bells, xylophone, marimba, vibraphone, plus sound-effects instruments, such as cymbals, tambourines, whistles, and ratchets.

THE PATH TO THE PHILHARMONIC

When he started college at the Eastman School of Music in Rochester, New York, Chris wasn't sure what kind of a percussionist he wanted to be. For a while during college, he was in a funk and jazz band. "I wanted to quit school and go on the road playing jazz," he says. But he didn't quit. He soon realized that what he loved most was playing in a symphony orchestra because of "the variety of instruments. With every concert, you play different instruments. In one performance I may play snare drums. In the next I'll play xylophone and cymbals."

CONCERT WATCH

It's fun to keep track of the number of instruments percussionists play in a concert. You'll also notice they do a fair amount of sitting around, waiting to play. They aren't napping while they wait—they're counting! They know the number of measures in the music when they don't have to play. They keep count so they'll be sure to come in again at exactly the right time. Philharmonic musicians usually count in their heads. In student orchestras, sometimes you can see percussionists moving their lips as they count off the measures silently. "Even if all you play is a single little note on a triangle, a lot of practice and preparation goes into it," says Chris Lamb. "The way you strike the instrument matters. How long the stick strikes the instrument and how it leaves the instrument affect how it sounds."

In 1985 he joined the New York Philharmonic as its principal percussion player, after being in two other orchestras for a few years. As the principal player, he decides which members of the percussion section play which instruments in a piece. Several weeks before a concert, he studies the music. "Then I create a road map," he says. He might have one person play marimba in the first section and then move over to play a triangle in the next section. Another may handle the bass drum in one section and the snare drum in the next. "You try to make it so that nobody bumps into anyone and people aren't running all over." To remember where he's supposed to go next in a piece, he'll write notes on the music. "I might draw a triangle, and that lets me know I'm supposed to move to the triangle next."

Chris demonstrates one of the instruments he created for the Concerto for Water Percussion, a piece composer Tan Dun (right) wrote for Chris to play with the New York Philharmonic.

Practicing is still something Chris enjoys doing each day, tapping away on the wide range of instruments he has in his basement at home or in his office at the Manhattan School of Music in New York City, where he teaches several days a week. Along with instruments for the orchestra, he has drums from South America, Asia, and Africa. "I like exploring the sounds of drums from other cultures," he says. "When the Philharmonic goes on tour to another country, I enjoy finding new instruments and learning new styles of drumming."

He has also created some instruments of his own. A Chinese composer named Tan Dun wrote a piece for Chris to play with the Philharmonic. The piece is about water. The composer wanted Chris to create instruments that would make the sound of water.

Chris had magical new instruments built out of tubes, bottles, buckets, and bowls. He used seventy-five gallons of water in the performance. "That's what I like about percussion, the variety," he says. "I like being active, just like when I was a kid."

Cynthia Phelps (front row left, with curly hair) with her four sisters, who all became professional musicians when they grew up: One sister plays piano, two are violinists, and one is a cellist.

Cynthia Phelps
Viola

Age when she started viola: 11 (started violin at 4; studied piano briefly in junior high)
Favorite books as a kid: *A Wrinkle in Time* and other books by Madeleine L'Engle
Other activities as a kid: Swimming, cheerleading, student council, drill team, dancing, babysitting
Other activities now: Running, reading, playing with her kids
Grew up in: Hollywood, California
Education: University of Southern California; University of Michigan
Before the Philharmonic: San Diego Symphony Orchestra; Minnesota Orchestra
Joined New York Philharmonic: 1992 as Principal Viola
Music she listens to now when relaxing: Jazz

"There was always so much music in my house all the time. My mother is a violinist. All four of my sisters play instruments. I always knew I wanted to be a musician. There was never a question about that," says Cynthia Phelps. But there was a question about something else: Which instrument was right for her?

"I started violin at age four," she says. "After a few years it was clear I was unhappy. I didn't enjoy making a sound on

INSIDE SCOOP: VIOLA

GOOD POINTS: "The viola's velvety sound is gorgeous," says Cynthia Phelps. "Sometimes violas have solos in a piece. Often violas play the melody. But a lot of times, violas play the support role in an orchestra instead of the main melody. It's very rewarding to support the melody, to weave in and out and make it shine." Another good point: Violas are smaller than cellos and easier to carry around.

BAD POINTS: "A viola is a little clumsy to hold," she adds. "It's bigger and heavier than a violin, but you have to hold it up like a violin instead of holding it down, as with a cello, which would be a more natural position. The strings are thicker than on a violin. It's harder to press them, which makes it harder to play in tune. I'm glad I had good early training on a violin so I had the strength and flexibility in my fingers to be able to play a viola in tune more easily."

the violin." However, there was an instrument whose sound she liked: the cello that an older sister played. "My mom figured out that the sound of the violin was just too high for me. I tended to like lower-sounding things, like cello."

So did Cynthia switch to cello? No! Her sister already played cello.

"I think the idea was to have a string quartet in the family," Cynthia explains. There are four instruments in a string quartet: one cello, two violins, and a viola. Cello was already taken, and two other sisters played violin. But nobody played viola—yet. A viola is bigger than a violin and has a lower sound but isn't as big or low-sounding as a cello. "My mother said if I kept playing the violin until I was big enough to hold a viola, then I could switch to viola. That bothered me at first. I probably sneaked in to play my sister's cello a little, but it wasn't a big deal. I was pretty agreeable to wait for the viola." But would she really like it?

"A RICH, VELVETY SOUND"

The summer before seventh grade, when Cynthia was eleven years old, her arms and hands were finally big enough to handle a viola. She gave it a try. She had no trouble figuring out how to play. "You hold a viola the same as a violin," she explains. "It's just that the viola is bigger so your arm goes out longer and your fingers have to stretch farther on the strings." Because of all those years of violin playing, her fingers knew just what to do.

"It was amazing how viola was a perfect fit for me," she says. "I could draw a good sound out of it right away. It had a rich, velvety sound that really appealed to me. I loved it."

When she returned to school that fall, her orchestra teacher noticed how much better Cynthia was on viola than she had been on violin. "The teacher asked if I worked hard all summer," Cynthia recalls. "It wasn't that I worked so hard, it was that I was working now with the kind of sound I liked. I could expand it into colors that were interesting and attractive to my ears. That inspired me."

She began to listen to recordings of pieces that made the most of the wonderfully warm tone of the viola. A favorite was Concerto for Orchestra by Hungarian composer Béla Bartók. "I used to babysit for our next-door neighbor, and they had a recording of it. When I babysat, I would put on the Bartók and play it over and over. It really grabbed me." She had a chance to learn great pieces like that in her school's orchestra, as well as in a youth orchestra that rehearsed on Saturdays, and also when she performed with the orchestra at the music camp she went to in the summer.

"MY OWN PERSON"

Cynthia was always good about practicing, even while struggling on violin. "It was part of our family life," she explains. "We got up early and practiced before school so that after school we had time for homework and after-school activities. People asked my mom how she got us to practice. She *made* us! A lot of parents don't want to do that, but it's important." Cynthia and her sisters took lessons from private teachers, but their mom, who was a violin teacher herself, helped them practice.

PRACTICE TIPS

IN THE GROOVE: "It helps if practicing becomes an expected part of your daily routine," says Cynthia Phelps. As a kid, she got into the habit of practicing at the same time each day. That makes it easier to remember to do it. If your afternoons are crazy with sports and lots of homework, maybe try what Cynthia did: practice in the morning before school.

IF YOU DON'T WANT TO PRACTICE: "Try to do at least fifteen minutes," suggests Cynthia Phelps. Music-making muscles stay in better shape if you use them regularly—even just a little each day—rather than skipping several days and trying to make up for it later with a superlong session.

"When I started viola, I remember thinking, Mom can't practice with me so much anymore because she can't read viola music." Viola music is written on a page differently than violin music. "I began to take more responsibility for my own practicing and my own approach to the instrument. Starting viola opened up a new world to me. I

Cynthia performs with the New York Philharmonic.

started to blossom as my own person, with my own voice."

"WANDER IN DREAMLAND"

"I didn't practice an excessive amount," she adds. "It was never more than an hour in the morning and an hour after school. I don't feel other areas of my life were ignored because of music. I grew up in Southern California and was outdoors a lot, playing with my sisters or neighborhood kids. I was on the student council. In

Cynthia shares a joke at a rehearsal with the Philharmonic's concertmaster, Glenn Dicterow.

high school, I was a cheerleader. I did the split and cartwheels, but our cheerleading was more like jazz dancing than gymnastics."

Another activity she squeezed into her busy days was reading. "I was such a bookworm. It was an escape to go places through books that I couldn't actually be in, to think things that didn't originate from my own head. Reading let me wander in dreamland. It also

helped me learn to concentrate. The freedom that reading released in me is something like what I feel when I
play music. I still like to read. So do other orchestra
members. I can always count on a recommendation of
a good book from my fellow musicians."

THE PATH TO THE PHILHARMONIC

"After high school, I went to a college instead of a
music conservatory because I wanted a broad education," she explains. The schools she went to are strong
in music: the University of Southern California and
then the University of Michigan. "I majored in music
performance but also took courses in art, psychology,
history, whatever I could fit in. By then, I was practicing five hours a day."

At first she thought she wanted to have a career
playing in orchestras that make soundtracks for
movies, like her high school viola teacher, who played
in the Walt Disney Studios orchestra. During her first
year at college, Cynthia played in movie orchestras on
the side. But soon she decided they weren't for her. She
felt movie music wasn't as interesting as the classical
music she was playing in college.

After finishing her college studies, she won several
important viola competitions and then tried out for a
California orchestra, the San Diego Symphony Orchestra. She became its principal viola. A few years later,

CONCERT WATCH

At an orchestra concert, watch the bows viola players slide across the strings. Usually all the bows go in the same direction at the same time. People think a viola section sounds better if everyone in it moves the bow the same way. That's also true for an orchestra's other string sections: the cellos, basses, first violins, and second violins. In each of these sections, the musicians usually move their bows up and down together. In a few pieces, members of a section may not bow together if some have different notes to play. But most of the time, all members of a string section play the same notes. Before the first rehearsal for a piece, the concertmaster and the principals in each string section decide how the bows are supposed to move in that piece, and directions are written down on each string player's copy of the music.

she moved to the Minnesota Orchestra. Then, in 1992, she became the New York Philharmonic's principal viola. All along, she has been playing chamber music, too, performing in string quartets or other small groups.

In addition to practicing viola every day, she now tries to run twenty miles a week. Squeezing everything in is tough because she's a working mom, with two young daughters: One is learning to play piano, and the other is studying cello. Cynthia's husband plays cello, too, with chamber music groups. Is Cynthia ever tempted to play their cellos? After all, that's what she wanted to play as a kid. "As a joke, sometimes I sit down and draw out a sound on cello and make everybody laugh," she says. "But cello is really different, even though it's a string instrument. Cello is fingered differently than viola and held differently. I couldn't switch. Besides, I'm happy with viola. I still love its deep, rich sound."

Jerry Ashby makes a hit at music camp, where campers didn't have to practice music all the time but also had a chance to play some baseball.

JEROME ASHBY
French Horn

Age when he started horn: 13 (started violin at 10)
Pets he had as a kid: Dogs named Queenie and Duchess
Pets he has now: Cats named Muffin, Blackie, and Sarah
Favorite books as a kid: Books about dogs
Other activities as a kid: Little League, collecting baseball cards and comics, playing stickball and handball with neighborhood kids, dog-walking
Other activities now: Spending time with his kids, trying new restaurants, watching baseball games and sometimes playing baseball, too
Grew up in: New York City
Education: The Juilliard School
Before the Philharmonic: Mexico City's Philharmonic Orchestra
Joined New York Philharmonic: 1979 as Associate Principal Horn
Teaches at: The Juilliard School; Manhattan School of Music; Curtis Institute of Music; Aspen Music Festival
Music he listens to now when relaxing: Classical

"Where I grew up, it wasn't that cool to walk home carrying a violin case," says Jerry Ashby. "My friends would rib me. I ignored them. It helped that I was very good in sports. I'd put the violin down when I got home and go out and play ball with those kids. I played stickball, handball, all the street games kids play in New York City. I was in Little League, too."

IN THE BRASS FAMILY

INSIDE SCOOP: FRENCH HORN

GOOD POINTS: "The rich, mellow sound is the best part," says Jerry Ashby. "The French horn gets to play beautiful solos in an orchestra." He likes that there are usually only four horn players in an orchestra, compared with about thirty violinists. Each hornist's playing stands out a little more than that of each violinist's. "You get to be more the center of attention in some ways."

BAD POINTS: "It's hard to learn to play the right notes," he adds. A horn player can make many different notes by holding down just one key. Which note comes out depends on how tight or relaxed the musician's lips are. That's true of other brass instruments, too, but getting exactly the right note is a little harder on horn than on trumpet or trombone.

Jerry had started violin in fifth grade, when kids at his New York City school could pick an instrument for the school orchestra. The orchestra had only string instruments. Jerry decided to try violin. "It was fun," he says. He even liked practicing every day, after he had slammed some hits in those neighborhood games. Soon he was playing violin in a special string orchestra on Saturdays. It was made up of the best elementary school musicians in the city. "I liked that orchestra. I was sort of shy. Being in that orchestra was a good way to make new friends."

In junior high, Jerry won a spot in the special Saturday orchestra for older students. But this one wasn't just for strings; it was a full orchestra, with wind and brass instruments, too. "That's where I first heard a French horn," Jerry says. "Its low, mellow sound seemed to call out to me. Some kids in the orchestra let me try their horns." Jerry was hooked. He wanted to switch to French horn. He told his school music teacher. But the teacher wouldn't let him. He said Jerry's lips were the wrong shape for French horn. "I kept bugging him. Finally he said I could take a French horn home to try over the summer." The teacher probably thought Jerry would be so frustrated he'd stick with violin.

"ALL I WAS INTERESTED IN"

"That summer, I was able to make a good sound on the French horn," Jerry says. "It seemed easier to me than violin. I felt I could express more of my personality when I played it. The sound really appealed to me."

What about his lips? The teacher turned out to be wrong about the kind of lips a French horn player was supposed to have. There are a lot of other *supposed-to* statements that people make that turn out not to be true—in music, sports, and other fields as well. If people really love a sport or an instrument, as Jerry did, they'll find a way to play it, no matter what anyone says.

Jerry took lessons all that first summer with an English teacher from his junior high who played French

PRACTICE TIPS

MAKE IT BEAUTIFUL: "I've heard people say études aren't interesting, but I've always enjoyed playing them," says Jerry Ashby. An étude is an exercise that helps a musician practice technical skills. "If you think of an étude as music and play it like beautiful music, it doesn't feel like an exercise. Try to sound as if you're singing through your instrument, no matter what you play. Even scales can be beautiful if you play them like they're real music."

IF YOU DON'T WANT TO PRACTICE: If you like music but you don't practice, maybe you haven't found the right instrument. "The sound has to call out to you," says Jerry Ashby. Keep your ears open at concerts or at rehearsals in school. Maybe another instrument's sound will call out to you.

horn ("horn" for short). By fall, Jerry was good enough to be the top horn player in his school band. He made it into the all-city youth orchestra, too. "That was the end of violin for me," says Jerry. It was also the end of team sports. He quit Little League to have time to practice horn. But he still played pickup games with friends. It was also the end of something else he had dreamed about when he was younger: becoming a veterinarian. He had always loved reading about dogs, had dogs as pets, and worked sometimes as a neighborhood dog-walker. "Once I picked up French horn, that's all I was interested in," says Jerry.

He stopped collecting baseball cards and comics. Instead, he collected albums of classical music. The first recording he bought was of Beethoven's Fifth Symphony, which has a gorgeous section of French horn playing. "I listened to that album so much I wore it out."

"HEAR THE NOTE IN YOUR HEAD"

After that first summer, his English teacher asked a friend who was a professional horn player to take over being Jerry's teacher. The new teacher played horn along with Jerry in their lessons. "That gave me an idea of what a horn could sound like. I would try to imitate him," says Jerry. "That kind of teaching is important for a beginner. French horn is beautiful, but it's hard to play the right note. By pressing one key, you can make twenty different notes. Which note you play depends on how you use your mouth. You play higher notes by making the lips tighter. For lower notes, you relax the lips. You have to hear the note in your head before you can play it."

Jerry's family didn't have much money. His mom wasn't a musician, but she saw how important music was to him. She found a way to pay for his lessons and also to rent a horn from a music store. After a year or so, she managed to buy him his own horn. That's what many families do: They rent first and don't buy an instrument until it's clear a kid is serious about music.

"AN ATHLETE IN TRAINING"

Jerry practiced every day after school for several hours. "I always liked practicing horn," he says. His dogs liked it, too. "When I played, they'd come closer. Practicing every day is important. With brass instruments, if you take a day off, it takes another day or two to get the muscles in your mouth back to where they were. It's like being an athlete in training. The more you

Jerry plays French horn with the New York Philharmonic.

practice, the better you get, and the more fun the instrument becomes."

For high school, he went to a public school that specialized in music and the arts. Every summer, he went to music camp in Massachusetts. "Camp was fantastic," he says. Not only did he improve on horn (and play baseball with other campers), but he also liked taking field trips to the nearby Tanglewood Music Festival, where the Boston Symphony Orchestra plays each summer. "Hearing that orchestra play on those beautiful grounds was really something. It was very motivating."

Jerry teaches one of his students at the Curtis Institute of Music in Philadelphia.

THE PATH TO THE PHILHARMONIC

However, there was another orchestra he had his heart set on joining, his "hometown team," the New York Philharmonic (the Phil for short). For college, he went

CONCERT WATCH

Sometimes you'll see French horn players roll their curly instruments upside down and shake them. There's a lot of metal tubing curled up in a French horn—about twenty feet. When musicians blow air into their horns, they also blow in some spit. If too much moisture collects inside a horn's tubing, the horn will make a fuzzy, gurgling sound. So they take off the horn's mouthpiece or part of the instrument's tubing and turn the horn upside down to let the spit drip out onto the floor. Other brass players empty out spit, too. Trumpeters and trombonists press a latch on their instruments' tubing. Tuba players pull out a small section of tubing and shake the moisture onto the floor. *Drip, drip, splat!*

to the Juilliard School in New York City. After graduating, he played for a while with an orchestra in Mexico. Soon he was ready to try out for the Phil, and he won the job of being its associate principal horn. "I felt like I'd won the lottery," he says. When not performing with the Phil, he teaches at several conservatories. "I usually teach in the afternoon. So I practice first thing every morning. A famous pianist once said, 'If I miss one day, I know it; if I miss two days, my wife knows it; and if I miss three days, everybody knows it.' I'd rather be ready than play catch-up."

He's still a baseball fan and watches games on TV. "I don't go to many games, however, because my kids always want to leave after the fourth inning," he says. He has even played pickup games with other Philharmonic musicians. "We used to play other orchestras that we met when we performed in other cities."

What Jerry likes most about the Philharmonic is what he likes best about playing ball. "I like the teamwork," he says. "An orchestra is like organized sports. You can't do it by yourself. You depend on the musicians next to you. You all have to work together."

*Mindy Kaufman started flute to be different from her twin brother, who
played clarinet. He didn't stick with music, but Mindy did.*

Mindy Kaufman
Flute

Age when she started flute: 8 (started piano at 7)
Pet she had as a kid: Cat named Poo
Pet she has now: Dog named Murphy
Favorite books as a kid: *The Boxcar Children* by Gertrude Warner; *Little Women* by Louisa May Alcott; *Old Possum's Book of Practical Cats* by T. S. Eliot
Other activities as a kid: Ice skating, Girl Scouts, skiing, teaching herself to play guitar
Other activities now: Biking, camping, hiking, working out at a gym, skiing, growing orchids
Grew up in: White Plains, New York
Education: Eastman School of Music
Before the Philharmonic: Rochester Philharmonic
Joined New York Philharmonic: 1979, playing piccolo and flute
Music she listens to now when relaxing: Latin, jazz

When she was about nine years old, Mindy Kaufman dreamed of being a champion ice skater. "I'd go to the ice rink with my friends a few afternoons a week," she says. "I took lessons and learned how to do jumps. I loved figure skating."

But there was something else she was starting to love even more. "I dreamed about being a figure skater for maybe a year. But I wasn't really all that serious about it. I was becoming much more involved in music."

She had been taking piano lessons since she was seven. "I enjoyed piano. I liked tinkering around on

INSIDE SCOOP: FLUTE

GOOD POINTS: "A flute is light and easy to carry," says Mindy Kaufman. "Flutes aren't too expensive, and inexpensive ones are playable. It's easy to make a sound on flute right away (although it can take years to make a really good sound, but that's true with any instrument). The sound is so beautiful."

BAD POINTS: "There are a lot of flutists so there's a lot of competition to get a job, or even into a youth orchestra," she notes. "It takes a large amount of air to play flute. When I was young, a few times I got light-headed until I learned to control my breath better. It's also an awkward instrument to hold, with your arms up in the air." To keep from hurting her muscles, "I don't practice for too long each day. If I have a pain when I practice, I stop and pay attention to it. I also try to sit well." That's good advice for preventing injuries with any instrument.

it," she says. She also liked the prizes her piano teacher gave. If Mindy memorized three pieces, her teacher gave her a small statue of a composer such as Ludwig van Beethoven. "Soon I had statues all over the place," she says. "That was fun."

At age eight, kids at her school could pick an instrument to play in the school band. She was doing so well on piano that she wanted to try another instrument. She also wanted to be different from her twin brother. He picked clarinet. "So I decided on flute, even though I didn't really know what it sounded like," she says. She started taking flute lessons with other kids at school. Once she began those lessons, she found that she loved the flute's high, floating sound. "I also liked being in the band with my friends," she says.

"With piano, I was mainly practicing and playing by myself. There aren't as many opportunities for young kids to play piano with other people." She kept on with piano and became pretty good at it. But she became even better on flute. "I seemed more drawn to the flute. I liked piano, but I *loved* flute."

"WONDERFUL TEACHERS"

All through elementary school, Mindy continued taking flute lessons at school. By junior high, she was so good the school music teacher didn't know enough about the instrument to help her anymore. He said she needed a private flute teacher. Her parents weren't musicians and didn't know any private teachers. But they knew of a nearby music school where kids could take lessons after school and on Saturdays. Mindy won scholarships to take both flute and piano lessons there.

"We didn't have money for lessons, and so it was lucky that this school gave me a scholarship," she says. "I really liked the school. It was in a big, old house." In addition to lessons, she took classes there in writing music and in music theory, which helps you learn more about how music is put together. "My Girl Scout leader was one of the music theory teachers. She was fun. It's so important to have a teacher who makes it fun. Actually, I was lucky with all my teachers. I had wonderful teachers."

Her flute teacher taught Mindy a practice strategy she still uses: Practice slowly. "If you play through a piece fast when you don't have it quite perfect, you just cement in the mistakes," explains Mindy. "Then it's harder to correct the mistakes than if you started slowly and learned it properly." She began using a metronome, a little machine that clicks out a steady beat. It can click fast or slow. "Set the metronome at a slow speed and do a passage a few times slowly. Then gradually speed up the metronome. It might take a few weeks to get it right. You need patience." Mindy had plenty of patience. She didn't mind practicing. "It was something I liked to do."

"FRIENDS FOR LIFE"

She also liked making music with other kids. She was in band and orchestra at her regular school. She also played in two youth orchestras outside of school. During summers, she played in a youth orchestra at a nearby music camp. "I made friends in youth orchestras that have stayed my friends for life," she says.

"I was busy. By the time I was fourteen or fifteen, I was practicing a few hours a day. I was out a few afternoons a week with youth orchestra rehearsals. But I was organized and got my homework done."

PRACTICE TIP

FIX IT: "Don't just play through a piece without paying attention to it," says Mindy Kaufman. If there's a spot you keep stumbling on, stop and work on it so you can find ways to fix it. "Use your practice time wisely so you analyze what you do. Figure out for yourself what you need to work on." However, in addition to all the thinking and fixing that's part of practicing, Mindy feels kids should "have a good time with music," as she has always done, from messing around as a teenager playing Beatles tunes—while also making great friends (and great music) in out-of-school ensembles—to being a musician for movies and pop stars today.

Mindy adds that "I didn't have much time for hobbies. Sometimes I went skating and did some skiing." She also liked listening to music on the radio. She owned a few recordings, including one with a performance of her favorite orchestral piece: *Petrouchka* by Russian composer Igor Stravinsky. "I listened to *Petrouchka* over and over. It's so big and imaginative," she says. It also has a great flute part. She liked pop music, too, especially the Beatles. She taught herself to play guitar and picked out pop and folk tunes on it.

"DON'T BE RIDICULOUS"

Each year, Mindy tried out for her local all-city orchestra, which was made up of the best student musicians in her city. To get into this orchestra, students had to play a piece for a judge. Mindy did well in these competitions and won an all-city spot every year. "Most of the time I wasn't nervous when I performed, but once in a while I was. I was more nervous when I played a solo for my schoolmates in the school auditorium than when I had to play in a competition for a judge. I found the best way to handle nerves is to be really prepared."

However, one competition made her almost quit music. Toward the end of high school, she tried out for New York's all-state orchestra. To get into it, students had to earn a perfect score of one hundred from the judge. Mindy played well in the tryout. She earned one hundred. Even so, the judges didn't let her in the

Watch an orchestra's flutes as they sparkle in the lights. Are they made of gold, silver, or wood? "Gold flutes, silver flutes, and wood flutes have slightly different sounds," says Mindy Kaufman. "For example, a gold flute has a more compact, laser-like sound, while a silver flute has a more round sound. Of course, this is my description. If you ask thirty flutists, you'll get thirty different answers!" Gold flutes are also heavier and can be more expensive than silver ones. The type of flute used depends mainly on the kind of sound a flutist likes. "My flute is silver," Mindy says. "But my headjoint [where the mouth goes] is made of gold." Her tiny piccolo is made of wood. In many concerts, she has to switch back and forth between flute and piccolo. "When I play one, either I put the other in my lap or on a table next to my chair. I don't put it on the floor because someone could step on it." Some woodwind and brass musicians stick their instruments onto a special stand during a performance when they're not in use.

all-state orchestra. She was so disappointed she told her school's band teacher she was not going to go into music. "Don't be ridiculous," he said. He explained that there were too many flutists that year who got a perfect score. There wasn't room for everyone in the orchestra. "Judges are not always right," she decided. "Thank goodness my teacher was level headed and gave good advice."

THE PATH TO THE PHILHARMONIC

Mindy didn't quit. Instead, for college she went to the Eastman School of Music in Rochester, New York. While a student there, she was hired to play flute with the Rochester Philharmonic. Then, in 1979, after graduation, she tried out for the New York Philharmonic and became one of its piccolo players. A piccolo

Some Philharmonic rehearsals are open to the public. These girls came to one with their school band. Afterward they met Mindy, who spoke with them about what it's like to be a musician.

is a small flute that is higher in tone than a regular flute. Now she plays both piccolo and flute with the Philharmonic. During her spare time, she occasionally plays backup music on albums for pop stars, such as Madonna. She also plays in orchestras that record soundtracks for movies, such as *Aladdin*. "It's fun to see the movie later and listen for the flute," she says.

Mindy continues to polish her flute-playing skills by practicing every day. A friend keeps her company—her dog, Murphy, who likes the sound of flute. "When I practice, Murphy sits right by my feet."

*Phil Smith plays a cornet while wearing his
Salvation Army uniform.*

PHILIP SMITH
Trumpet

Age when he started cornet: 7 (cornet is like a trumpet; switched to trumpet in eleventh grade)

Pets he had as a kid: Dogs named Rex and Duchess

Favorite books as a kid: Hardy Boys books

Other activities as a kid: Baseball, stickball, lacrosse

Other activities now: Walking; spending time with his kids; playing gospel music

Grew up in: Floral Park, New York (born in England)

Education: The Juilliard School

Before the Philharmonic: Chicago Symphony Orchestra

Joined New York Philharmonic: 1978 as Co-Principal Trumpet; became Principal Trumpet in 1988

Teaching: Has a few private students

Music he listens to now when relaxing: Gospel music, contemporary Christian pop music

A visit from the Tooth Fairy—that's what losing "baby teeth" means to many kids. But to Phil Smith, it meant that soon he could play the shiny instrument he'd been waiting to play for so long: a cornet, which is a kind of trumpet. Phil's dad played cornet. "I would fall asleep listening to him practice," Phil remembers. "He had a sweet, mellow tone."

Phil was born in England, where his dad was in the British army for a while, playing cornet in a military band. After leaving the military, his dad played in the brass bands that are a big part of his church, the Salvation Army.

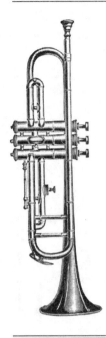

IN THE BRASS FAMILY

INSIDE SCOOP: TRUMPET

<u>GOOD POINTS:</u> "A trumpet is not as fragile as a string instrument," says Phil Smith. "You can play it outside and not worry about it cracking. If it gets a little dent, a repair person can get the dent out." It's light, easy to carry, and is a showy instrument—its sound stands out in any ensemble.

<u>BAD POINTS:</u> "It can be frustrating at the beginning," he adds. It takes a while to learn how to buzz your lips into the mouthpiece to make a sound. It also takes a while to get the hang of changing the pressure in your lips to play different notes with the same fingering. If you don't hit a note exactly right, it can sound bad. "It's good for kids to start on cornet, which makes a more mellow tone than trumpet. If you don't hit a note exactly right, your *blat* will sound better on cornet."

He kept playing in church bands after the family moved to New York when Phil was about six.

Phil was eager to play cornet, but his dad wanted to wait until Phil's new front teeth had grown in. To play a brass instrument like a cornet or trumpet, you press the mouthpiece against your lips. If there are no teeth behind the lips, you can't play. After Phil's seventh birthday, he finally had all his new front teeth. He started taking cornet lessons from his dad and was soon playing in church bands, too.

"A cornet is the same as a trumpet except for its shape," Phil explains. "It's more compact and easier for a kid to hold. It makes a softer, more mellow sound. At first, I played cornet because that was what you did in my family. It became something I liked for myself when I started hearing positive comments. I'd play in church and people would say, 'You sound so good.' When you get positive feedback like that, you think, 'Well, I'll keep on.' But I didn't practice much, not if I could help it."

"HATED PRACTICING"

"I hated practicing," says Phil. "I'd rather have been playing stickball and baseball." But his parents made sure he practiced most days. If he hadn't practiced by the time his dad got home from work, his dad would go down in the basement with Phil and they would practice together. "I'd usually end up in tears, with him being frustrated with me. It's often hard to study with your parents. But we didn't have enough money for me to study with anyone else. Plus, my father knew he could do it better." Phil's mom helped keep the peace by reminding Phil to practice *before* his dad came home.

However, nobody had to force Phil to go to the rehearsals or performances for the many music groups he was in. He loved *playing* in all kinds of ensembles. It was just practicing that he didn't like. Besides Salvation Army bands, he was always in his school concert band. In high school, he also joined the school jazz band, marching band, and orchestra. He liked sports,

PRACTICE TIPS

MATCH THAT SOUND: "Find a teacher who will play with you in lessons," says Phil Smith. "That's the best way to learn to make a good sound. That's how my dad taught me. He would play and then I would play. You hear a good sound that way, and then your brain and your ear work with your muscles so you can create that sound, too." Also, listen to recordings of great musicians playing your instrument. Eventually you'll add your own special touches to the sound you make so it's *your* sound and not just a copy of the people you've heard.

IF YOU DON'T WANT TO PRACTICE: "The hardest part for me about practicing is starting, walking down those basement stairs to my practice room," says Phil Smith. "But then I think about the piece I have to play in orchestra next week and I know I better get down there. Once I'm down there and start playing, it turns into a challenge: Can I get it? Hey, that sounds good. Let's see if I can do the next part." He takes breaks, too. "It's better for me to play for a while, go out for a walk, and then come back and play some more."

too, and played lacrosse for a while. "That ended when I got whacked in the mouth and almost lost a tooth, a big problem for a brass player. As much as I enjoyed lacrosse, I decided music was the way to go."

He and some high school friends also had fun playing in a rock band they called Uncle Phil. They performed music from 1960s rock bands such as Blood, Sweat & Tears. "I'd listen to their albums and write down the music for the brass section," says Phil. "I liked playing rock." He also liked brass band music. But he wasn't very interested in orchestra music yet.

A TRICKY SURPRISE

Up until eleventh grade, Phil played only cornet. Both cornet and trumpet are used in bands, but orchestras mainly use trumpets. In eleventh grade, his school music teachers persuaded him to start playing trumpet, too, in case he wanted to go on in music. "I figured I'd go to college and become a school music teacher," Phil recalls. However, a professional trumpet player heard Phil perform with a Salvation Army band. She said Phil was so good he should go to a top conservatory, like the Juilliard School. So he decided to try. However, to get into a school like Juilliard, trumpeters not only have to play well, they also need to have mastered some special skills used in orchestra music. "I knew nothing about that," says Phil.

He knew how to play the basic trumpet kids play in school, called the B-flat trumpet. However, there are many other kinds of trumpets. A lot of orchestra music is written for those other trumpets. If you don't have one of those other trumpets, that's okay. You can still play music written for them *if* you can figure out quickly—right on the spot—what the notes would be if they had been written for the trumpet you do have. That's called transposing. Phil had never heard of it.

✦ ✦ ✦

Phil sometimes teaches workshops for young trumpeters, as he's doing here.

"HAD A FIT"

Phil walked into his Juilliard tryout with his basic B-flat trumpet. He played a piece he had learned. He played well. The judges were impressed.

Then he was given music to play that he hadn't seen before. It was written for a C trumpet, a different kind of trumpet than the one Phil had. He didn't realize that. To play the music correctly using his B-flat trumpet, he would have to do some tricky on-the-spot transposing. He didn't realize that either. So he started playing. The man running the audition "had a fit," says Phil. The man explained that Phil was playing all the notes wrong. "I didn't know what he was talking about," adds Phil. Amazingly, he was accepted into Juilliard. But school officials wouldn't let him play in their orchestras until he learned to do transposing.

Phil worked hard at Juilliard. He practiced a lot. Not only did he have to master transposing and learn about classical music, but he also had to learn to make a more forceful, brassy sound. Even though he was playing trumpet, he made a mellow sound as if he were still playing cornet. By his third year at Juilliard, he had mastered both transposing and brassy playing. He had improved so much that he won a spot in a Juilliard orchestra.

◆ ◆ ◆

CONCERT WATCH

Sometimes a trumpeter sticks something into the big open end of the trumpet—a small, pear-shaped object called a mute. It makes the trumpet less loud and also changes the kind of sound a trumpet makes. There are many different mutes, such as straight mutes and cup mutes. There's a special one used in jazzy pieces: a Harmon mute, nicknamed a "wah-wah" mute. It has a hole in the end of it. If trumpeters move their left hand back and forth over the hole in this mute while blowing into the trumpet, they can make a *wah-wah* sound. Other brass instruments use mutes, too.

THE PATH TO THE PHILHARMONIC

After graduating from Juilliard, he won a job with the Chicago Symphony Orchestra, which had a terrific trumpet section. In 1978, he moved to the New York Philharmonic. At first he shared the job of principal trumpet with another musician. In 1988, he became the Philharmonic's principal trumpet all by himself.

He is famous for the range of tones he can make on a trumpet. He can blare out crisp, bold blasts that are needed in some parts of a symphony. For quieter sections, he uses a more mellow tone—a sound he learned to make from all those years of playing cornet as a kid. He also does something else he did as a kid. Sometimes he plays in Salvation Army bands, when not performing with the Philharmonic. In addition, he has fun playing in his own band that plays gospel music; his wife is the band's singer.

He practices about six days a week and finds time to

teach some students. He stresses with his students the importance of having a good tone and of "telling a story" with music. "Music is not just the black dots on the white paper," he says. "It's what happens when those black dots on the white paper go into your heart, and come out again."

*Sherry Sylar may have smiled nicely for the camera, but she
wasn't happy about taking piano lessons. Several years later, she
found an instrument that made her smile for real.*

Sherry Sylar

Oboe

Age when she started oboe: 12 (started piano at 6 and flute at 11)
Pet she had as a kid: Cat named Shasta (short for Shostakovich, a Russian composer)
Pet she has now: Cat named Luciano (Luchi, for short)
Favorite book as a kid: *Lord of the Rings* by J. R. R. Tolkein
Other activities as a kid: Girl Scouts, bike riding, softball, horseback riding, teaching herself guitar and picking out Beatles tunes on it
Other activities now: Yoga, hiking, cooking
Grew up in: Chattanooga, Tennessee
Education: Indiana University; Northwestern University
Before the Philharmonic: University of Evansville (teacher); Louisville Orchestra
Joined New York Philharmonic: 1984 as Associate Principal Oboe
Teaches at: Mannes College of Music; also has a few private students
Music she listens to now when relaxing: Jazz

"When I was about four years old, I started plunking out tunes on the piano," says Sherry Sylar. "So my parents started me on piano lessons at age six." But Sherry and piano lessons didn't mix well. She took lessons at a music conservatory. Some kids might like that, but not Sherry. "It was a very formal place. I was kind of shy. It was scary to go there," she remembers. Also, the teacher had Sherry play mostly scales and exercises. "That didn't capture my attention. I wanted to play cool music. I was not good about practicing. It was a chore to make me do it."

INSIDE SCOOP: OBOE

GOOD POINTS: "The oboe often plays beautiful solos in an orchestra or band," says Sherry Sylar. Although oboe was a popular instrument at her junior high, usually not as many kids play oboe as other instruments, such as flute or clarinet. So there's a better chance of getting into a youth orchestra if you play oboe. Another good point: the sound. "I still love it," she says.

BAD POINTS: "It's harder to make a sound on oboe than on flute as a beginner," she adds. "You also need to be mature enough to take care of the reeds. They're fragile. At first you'll probably buy them. They can cost as much as twenty dollars each. You should be making your own reeds within the first year or you'll go broke. You not only need musical talent to play oboe, you have to be good at making things." The oboe is called a double-reed instrument because each reed consists of two sticks of bamboo tied together. When blown on, the reeds vibrate against each other, letting the oboe make a sound.

But still she liked music, especially singing. In Girl Scouts, she always led the troop in singing songs. She also liked doing crafts in Scouts. What a surprise when she discovered an instrument that combined crafts *and* a glorious singing sound!

She made that discovery in junior high school. At lunchtime one day, she heard funny squeaking noises coming from the band teacher's office. Sherry peeked in and saw the teacher carving away at a long piece of bamboo. She was turning it into tiny sticks, called reeds, for an instrument called an oboe. To test the reeds as she was making them, the teacher put them in her mouth and made little peeping sounds. However, when she finished a set of reeds and put them onto her wooden oboe, she made a wonderfully musical tone that sounded like someone singing or humming. "I fell in love with the sound," says Sherry. "It was fascinating to watch her make reeds. She let me help." That did it: a singing sound and a craft project, too. "I told her I had to play oboe."

THE RIGHT SOUND

At first, the junior high band teacher didn't want Sherry to play oboe. The school band already had oboe players. When Sherry had joined her school's ensemble at the start of junior high, she began playing flute because the band needed flutists. But Sherry didn't really like flute and didn't practice much. She made it clear to her teacher that oboe was what she wanted.

So the teacher gave her a few reeds and an old oboe to try at home. "It was this plastic thing that didn't have all the keys that a normal oboe has. It was a really bad beginner's instrument," remembers Sherry. "Maybe the teacher was trying to discourage me. But they couldn't get me to stop practicing that oboe. It made the kind of sound I wanted to hear. Within six months, my parents bought me a good, wooden oboe. They thought that any kid who comes home and practices two hours a day on this squeaky plastic thing is determined to play."

Sherry started taking private oboe lessons with the band teacher. These worked out better than the piano lessons. Kids need a teacher they feel comfortable with,

PRACTICE TIP

<u>IF YOU DON'T WANT TO</u> <u>PRACTICE:</u> "Take a popular piece of music you like and try to pick out the notes so you can play it on your instrument," suggests Sherry Sylar. "That gets you playing the instrument and can help get you started if you're having trouble making yourself practice. It's fun." She figured out Beatles songs by listening to recordings. If you'd rather use written music, look for books of pop tunes in music stores.

and this time Sherry lucked out. Not only were the lessons at places where Sherry felt relaxed (either at the teacher's house or at the junior high), but the teacher picked pieces Sherry found exciting: oboe solos from real symphonies. "The teacher also had me practice scales and études," says Sherry. "I didn't regard them as a chore as I had with piano. I wanted to get really good on technical things, like playing fast notes." Sherry didn't mind practicing because "I just loved that sound."

"A GOOD GIRL SCOUT BIT THE DUST"

"When I started oboe, a good Girl Scout bit the dust," says Sherry. She quit Scouts to have time to practice oboe several hours each afternoon and also keep up with homework. "I did well in school. Music developed my sense of discipline." She quit softball, too, and flute. She also stopped piano lessons. But she had to admit that piano had been helpful. "Piano is the best background for learning other instruments. Going into band was easier because I knew how to read music from my six years of piano lessons." All that tapping away at the piano's keys helped, too, by getting her fingers ready for the fast fingering needed for oboe.

Her fingers were also learning how to do something

else—carve bamboo poles into reeds. Ready-made oboe reeds can be bought in music stores, but store-bought reeds are expensive and don't actually work as well as ones oboists make for themselves. By high school, Sherry was making her own reeds.

"WITH OTHER KIDS"

All through high school, Sherry played oboe in many groups. "There was nothing more fun than being part of a band or orchestra, to be with other kids and play great music," she says. "I was in marching band and loved playing at football games, but the marching routines were a challenge." She also played in her school's concert band, joined a youth orchestra, went to music camp, and performed sometimes at the church where her mom was the organist. Sherry also entered competitions and won a spot in Tennessee's all-state orchestra.

She found time for other kinds of fun, too. She went horseback riding with a friend who had a horse. Sherry and another friend taught themselves to play guitar. "I'd pluck out Beatles songs on guitar and on oboe, too. I wasn't listening to much classical music. I was more into the Beatles and pop music."

THE PATH TO THE PHILHARMONIC

For college, Sherry majored in music performance at Indiana University. Then she taught music for a few years at another university in Indiana, while playing in

CONCERT WATCH

Right before a concert starts, the concertmaster points to the principal oboe, who usually sits near the middle of the orchestra. The oboist plays a note—an A. Then the other musicians play that same note. If their notes aren't exactly the same as the oboist's, they make some adjustments on their instruments. "Oboes lead the tuning because we're centrally located and make a loud sound that everyone can hear easily," says Sherry Sylar. She serves as principal oboe when the regular principal isn't there. To be ready to play that note, she uses a small electronic device called a tuner. It plays a perfect A. She makes sure her oboe plays exactly like the tuner.

local orchestras. Next, she studied at Northwestern University in Illinois with an oboist from the Chicago Symphony Orchestra. Then she landed a job with the Louisville Orchestra in Kentucky. A few years later, in 1984, she won the job of associate principal oboe with the New York Philharmonic. Along with performing in the Philharmonic, she also does chamber music and sometimes plays in orchestras that make soundtracks for movies.

Besides practicing every day, Sherry spends about ten hours a week making six to ten reeds. "Luckily, I can watch television while I make them," she says. She also likes to do yoga and go hiking. To unwind, she likes to cook, but not while listening to classical music. "I love classical music, but it's hard to listen to it without being critical. We have to be so critical of ourselves when we play that it's hard not to be critical of other classical performers, too. So to relax, I listen to jazz. I don't know much about jazz, but I like it."

Sherry teaches at the Mannes College of Music in New York City, but also has a few private students. She teaches them in a more re-laxed setting, in the

After a New York Philharmonic concert for kids, Sherry lets a few audience members hear an oboe close up.

kind of place where she would have liked to study as a kid: her house in the country. "Luchi, my cat, enjoys interrupting my lessons by opening the door to my studio, twining around my student's legs, and jump-ing on my shoulders. He has been known to sit in my lap while I practice, but *not* when I practice very high notes. Those make him run the other way."

Sherry shows how to make a peeping sound on oboe reeds.

Judy LeClair dances with her dog, Sherlock.

Judith LeClair

Bassoon

Age when she started bassoon: 11 (started piano at 8 and cello at 10)
Pet she had as a kid: Dog named Sherlock
Pet she has now: Dog named Brillo
Favorite books as a kid: Mysteries
Other activities as a kid: Horseback riding, biking, running, babysitting, reading
Other activities now: Running, swimming, playing with her young son, taking photographs
Grew up in: Parkersburg, West Virginia, and Wilmington, Delaware
Education: Eastman School of Music
Before the Philharmonic: San Diego Symphony Orchestra; San Diego Opera Orchestra
Joined New York Philharmonic: 1981 as Principal Bassoon
Teaches at: The Juilliard School
Music she listens to now when relaxing: Jazz or whatever her young son puts on

"I had a record player when I was little," says Judy LeClair. "I remember listening to a record of *Peter and the Wolf*." It tells the story of a boy who disobeys his grandfather by going into a meadow, where he has a run-in with a wolf. Different instruments play the characters. For example, horns play the part of the wolf. The grandfather is played by a tall woodwind instrument called a bassoon. "I always liked the sound of the bassoon in *Peter and the Wolf*," Judy says. "The bassoon has a mellow, chocolate kind of a sound. I liked listening to it."

INSIDE SCOOP: BASSOON

GOOD POINTS: "A bassoon has a beautiful, mellow sound and is the backbone of the woodwind section," says Judy LeClair. "Just about every orchestra piece has an important part for bassoon." Although the bassoon has more than twenty-three keys and eight finger holes that you press in various combinations to make different notes, she says, "It was fun to learn the fingerings."

BAD POINTS: "A bassoon is big, almost five feet tall, and pretty heavy," she adds. "It's hard at first to learn to make a good sound. If you have bad reeds, it's hard to play." The bassoon is a double-reed instrument like an oboe. At first beginners buy reeds or borrow used ones from their teachers. Eventually you learn to make reeds "that will give you the kind of sound you want to make."

There were also other things she liked as a kid: playing with her dog, Sherlock, and riding horses. When she was seven, she scared her mom by being a bit of a daredevil and riding bareback on a neighbor's horse. So her mom had Judy take riding lessons.

Judy also tried to keep up with her older brother and sister. They were taking piano lessons from a teacher in a nearby town. So Judy did, too, starting at age eight. Then her brother began playing two really big instruments: a tuba, the largest brass instrument, and a bass, the largest string instrument. He played them in his school band and orchestra (and still plays them today). So Judy became interested in big instruments, too. Plus, playing music in school with other kids looked like more fun than practicing piano by herself. In fifth grade, she began taking lessons at school on a pretty big instrument, a cello. "I wasn't very good at cello," she says. "I didn't like using the bow and didn't learn the finger positions. I got frustrated with my scratchy sound. I wanted to play something different and *unusual*." In junior high, she found it.

"A FUN CHALLENGE"

Her West Virginia junior high school had an unusual instrument nobody was playing: a tall, skinny plastic tube with shiny keys. The band director asked Judy if she'd give it a try. It was a bassoon, the instrument whose sound she liked so much in *Peter and the Wolf*. It was nearly five feet high, almost as tall as she was. "It looked like a fun challenge," Judy says. "So I brought it home." She brought home some reeds, too. Bassoon reeds are something like oboe reeds, only bigger.

"That plastic bassoon was in terrible shape," she recalls. "Just getting it to play was a miracle. At first it was pretty awful sounding, but that didn't discourage me. I liked using air to make the sound instead of a bow. I liked the keys and the challenge of learning the fingerings. I practiced all the time." She played in her school band and took bassoon lessons from the school band director.

"THAT'S WHEN I KNEW"

"I started getting better at bassoon. In eighth grade, with some money I earned babysitting, I bought a student-model wooden bassoon," she says. "My band

PRACTICE TIPS

BUILD IT UP: "You can't build a house without a foundation, and you can't play music well without the basics," says Judy LeClair. As a kid, she started practice sessions by warming up with basics like scales and études. She also did "long tones"—choosing one note, gradually playing it louder and louder, and then, just as gradually, playing it more quietly. "Try to keep a steady stream of air, without wobbling. Do this with a different note each day. Hold it a little longer each time. I liked the challenge. Doing exercises like that makes you a stronger player."

IF YOU DON'T WANT TO PRACTICE: "Go hear a live concert or a recital," suggests Judy LeClair. "Recordings are fine, but if you hear someone play *live*, it's so exciting. You say, 'Wow, so that's what the instrument can do.'" Professional concerts or student performances might fire you up to practice more.

director at school realized there was nothing more he could teach me and suggested I study with a bassoon instructor at a nearby university." Her parents weren't musicians, but they, too, could tell that Judy had a special talent for this tall wooden instrument.

"The summer I turned fourteen, I went to music camp," Judy says. "That was the first time I played in an orchestra. I fell in love with it! That's when I knew I wanted to be a musician."

"PART OF A TEAM"

When Judy started high school, her family moved to Delaware. They heard of a good bassoon teacher in Philadelphia, Pennsylvania, not far from their new home. So Judy traveled to Philadelphia every Wednesday and Saturday. She not only took lessons but was also in a chamber music group with other kids at the music school where the teacher worked. "Playing chamber music really teaches you to listen, to blend your sound with others, to be part of a team," says Judy. "The other kids were so good. It was an exciting challenge to come up to their level. When I was sixteen, we won a competition to play a piece by Mozart with the Philadelphia Orchestra. That was one of the most exciting experiences I can remember!"

Judy was also in her high school band, but her heart was in Philadelphia, where she loved to spend her Saturdays. She was in a youth orchestra there on Saturday mornings, played chamber music in the afternoons, and sometimes stayed into the evening to hear a concert by the Philadelphia Orchestra.

Judy plays bassoon for youngsters at the preschool her son attended.

During summers, she went to music camp. She began learning to make reeds, too. "It was hard to find time for everything, but I managed. I got good grades, but my focus was music. I loved to practice. I wasn't much of a TV watcher. So after dinner I practiced every night until everyone went to sleep."

There was no time in that busy schedule for horseback riding. However, she feels riding as a kid helped her. "Riding is about concentration, rhythm, and focusing on details, just like music. A skill like horseback riding can help to develop your concentration."

CONCERT WATCH

Some musicians warm up on stage before a concert. This is especially true for instruments that use reeds, such as bassoon, oboe, and clarinet. "A reed changes depending on temperature and humidity," says clarinetist Pascual Martinez Forteza (whom you'll meet later in this book). "If you try a reed in the dressing room, when you get on stage the temperature may be different. We like to try a reed where we're going to play."

THE PATH TO THE PHILHARMONIC

After high school, Judy won a scholarship to go to college at the Eastman School of Music. When she graduated, she became the principal bassoon player for two orchestras in California. A short time later, in 1981, she became the New York Philharmonic's principal bassoon. In her spare time, she likes to play chamber music. "There are many great orchestra pieces that I love to play," she says. "But more than anything else, I love to play chamber music. It sharpens your skills and makes you part of a very intimate experience."

During her first years at the Philharmonic, she went back to horseback riding for a short while. But with all the practicing and rehearsing she had to do with the Philharmonic, plus taking care of two dogs and an old house, she didn't have time for riding. She married a pianist who teaches at Julliard. Now she has a new responsibility that keeps her busy when she's not playing with the Philharmonic: taking care of their young son. Even so, she finds time to share what she has learned about bassoon by teaching at Juilliard. "It's important that my students see that I'm a working mother. They need to see that there are important things in life other than making music or getting that one special job—that there is always a balancing act."

Joe Alessi fools around with a party hat, pretending he's playing trumpet like his father.

Joseph Alessi
Trombone

Age when he started trombone: 8 (started cornet at 5 and piano in sixth grade)
Pets he had as a kid: Dogs, including one named Bandit
Pets he has now: Cats named Milo and Chester
Favorite book as a kid: *Green Eggs and Ham* by Dr. Seuss
Other activities as a kid: Baseball, skiing
Other activities now: Golf, water skiing, playing basketball with his kids, performing in his own jazz band
Grew up in: San Rafael, California
Education: The Curtis Institute of Music
Before the Philharmonic: Philadelphia Orchestra; Montreal Symphony Orchestra
Joined New York Philharmonic: 1985 as Principal Trombone
Teaches at: The Juilliard School
Music he listens to now when relaxing: Jazz

"I started playing cornet when I was about five," says Joe Alessi. "It was almost expected of me to play cornet and trumpet. My father played trumpet in the San Francisco Symphony. My grandfather played trumpet, too, at the Metropolitan Opera in New York. Trumpet appealed to me. I heard it all the time at home."

Joe played cornet and trumpet for three years. His father was his teacher. That was both good and bad. "He was a good father in that he would sit down with me and help me, show

INSIDE SCOOP: TROMBONE

<u>GOOD POINTS:</u> "The most interesting thing about trombone is the slide," says Joe Alessi. "The slide makes it unique." There's a lot to learn about different ways to make sounds with the slide, including cool, swooping sounds. Another plus: It's not too hard for a beginner to make a sound.

<u>BAD POINTS:</u> "It's easy to overblow," he notes. It takes a while to learn to blow just right to make a really good sound. It also takes a while to get the hang of using the slide on this big, heavy instrument. "There's not as much good music written for trombone as for trumpet or horn," he adds. He encourages composers to write pieces with good trombone solos.

---

me what to do," Joe recalls. "He taught me how to practice, how to take a piece apart and practice it bit by bit. I got my work ethic from him. He was a hard worker all his life. Not practicing was not an option." But there was a downside to those lessons. "We had battles in the lessons. If I made a mistake, I'd hear about it. He'd yell, and I'd cry. Then he'd have to get me to dry up all the tears and go on. Those lessons were tough."

Even tougher was what happened when Joe was eight years old. "One day, my father came in with a trombone and asked if I wanted to play it," Joe says. "My father realized that a trumpet mouthpiece didn't fit my mouth that well. He knew I could play better on trombone. But I didn't want to have anything to do with trombone. I wanted to be a trumpet player, just like him. So he said he'd leave the trombone there and maybe someday I'd feel like picking it up. I was devastated."

"NO PROBLEM!"

Several weeks went by. Joe wouldn't touch that trombone. He kept tootling away on trumpet, but always struggled to hit the high notes. "One day, my father heard me struggling and said, 'Just try the trombone once, and I won't bother you about it again.' So I tried trombone. I went right up to a high B-flat on it, real strong. No problem!" His father was right. Joe *could* play trombone more easily than trumpet. Good-bye, trumpet—hello, trombone.

"My father found me a trombone teacher, a real calm, patient guy, unlike my father," says Joe. "The teacher came every week to our house and gave me lessons. Once I started studying with that teacher, it was easier to practice."

Joe was also busy with baseball. "I could hit the ball pretty well," he says. So could his father, who had almost been a pro ball player. "My father always had a way to get better at anything. To help me with hitting, he put up a punching bag with clothes in it. I would hit that bag with my bat fifty times a day." His father also had Joe take piano lessons in sixth grade. "I hated piano lessons," says Joe. "But for as little as I did on piano, it has paid off. I play trombone parts on piano to hear what they sound like. I use piano a lot today in my teaching."

Joe was doing well on trombone, playing in his elementary and junior high bands and in a school jazz band, too. He was also in a youth orchestra outside of school. "I liked the music in youth orchestra more than the music we played in school. I became interested in being in an orchestra because of that," he says. However, he wasn't practicing much. He still wasn't crazy about trombone.

"THE COOLEST THING"

Joe started becoming more of a trombone fan when he was about fourteen and his father brought home a special recording. "It was the coolest thing," Joe says. It was a recording of only trombones and tubas, played by members of the Chicago Symphony Orchestra. They were playing the trombone and tuba parts from famous orchestra pieces. That gave Joe a chance to hear how great trombones could sound when played by terrific musicians. Then a friend of his father's took Joe to a trom-

---

PRACTICE TIP

TRA-LA-LA: "Sing what you're practicing before you play it," advises Joe Alessi. "Singing helps because you have to have the rhythm and the pitches in your head before you pick up the instrument. You'll play more in tune and more rhythmically. A lot of people are afraid to sing, but give it a try. You could go 'ta—ta-ta-ta' or 'bah-bah-bah.' It doesn't matter." He also suggests *pretending* to play your instrument while you sing. Don't even hold it. Put your hands up as if you were playing, using imaginary keys, strings, slide, or bow. "Then when you pick up the real instrument, it's easier to play," he says. "I have my students do that."

bone convention in Tennessee. All kinds of trombonists were there, including one from the New York
Philharmonic. "I couldn't believe there were that
many people interested in trombone. They were just
nuts about it. Hearing them play was a big education
for me. I began to really like the sound of trombone."

One of his father's trumpet students gave Joe a
recording of J. J. Johnson, an amazing jazz trombonist.
"His sound was warm and rich. I wanted to sound that
way. From then on I was always listening to J. J. Johnson recordings. I started practicing three or four hours
a day."

Practice time at Joe's house was noisy. Everyone
practiced at once, including the dog. His older brother
and father played trumpet. His mom was a singer. His
dog Bandit was a "singer," too. He howled whenever
he heard a trumpet. But Bandit didn't mind the sound
of a trombone.

"KEEP GOING"

By the time Joe was in high school, he was having fun
performing in all kinds of groups: school bands, a
youth orchestra, a brass quintet with college kids, and
a jazz band with one of his father's students. Joe also
regularly won spots in California's all-state ensembles.
During his first year in high school he also won a special competition for young musicians. "That inspired

"I love to teach," Joe says. Besides teaching college-age musicians at Juilliard, he sometimes teaches workshops for young brass players.

me to keep going," he says. The prize was a chance to perform with the San Francisco Symphony and have a vacation in Europe.

"In high school, my academic teachers understood that my emphasis was music, and they were easy on me," says Joe. When his brass quintet played concerts during the school day, Joe says, "I would be excused from class to go do this. I let my homework slide sometimes."

At the end of his junior year in high school, a trombone job opened up in the San Francisco Ballet's orchestra. "My father said I should try out for it. I won

Joe encourages a young trombonist to take a big breath.

the job. I was just sixteen. That summer I went to summer school and took the rest of the courses I needed to graduate from high school. During what would have been my senior year of high school I had this job, which was great. I earned money that I saved up for college."

THE PATH TO THE PHILHARMONIC

For college, Joe went to a conservatory, the Curtis Institute of Music in Philadelphia, Pennsylvania. He played mainly classical music there, but he had fun

CONCERT WATCH

At an orchestra concert, count the number of trombone players on stage. Then count the violinists. There are more violinists, right? There are more cellists and violists, too. Many composers don't want more than four trombones in their symphonies. Trombones are loud. Too many would make it hard to hear the strings. Usually there aren't more than four French horns, four flutes, or four of each of the other brass and woodwind instruments either. There are exceptions. Composer Gustav Mahler included ten French horns in one symphony. But Wolfgang Amadeus Mozart and Ludwig van Beethoven wrote some symphonies with no trombones at all.

performing with jazz groups on the side. After graduating, he was in orchestras in Philadelphia and Montreal and then joined the New York Philharmonic in 1985 as its principal trombone. When not playing with the Philharmonic, he teaches at the Juilliard School, performs in a brass quintet, and gives workshops for young trombonists. "I try to practice every day," he says. "It's not always fun. But if you don't, you won't play as well."

Shortly after joining the Philharmonic, he met his jazz hero, J. J. Johnson, who was playing in a jazz club in New York City. Joe went to hear him at the club, and they became friends. Later, Joe played with him on the last recording Johnson made before he died in 2001. "I'm not the greatest at jazz," says Joe. "But I'm pretty decent. It's something I want to study more."

He loves playing jazz in the band he started: Joe's Jersey Jazz Jesters.

Joe has come a long way from his first less-than-enthusiastic meeting with a trombone when he was eight. "I had to grow into liking trombone. Now I love it."

Hai-Ye Ni playing cello at her school in Shanghai, China.

HAI-YE NI
Cello

Age when she started cello: 7 (started violin at 4)
Favorite books as a kid: Mysteries
Other activities as a kid: Ping-Pong, reading, drawing
Other activities now: Biking, walking, swimming, reading
Grew up in: Shanghai, China, and San Francisco, California
Education: San Francisco Conservatory of Music; the Juilliard School
Before the Philharmonic: Soloist and chamber musician
Joined New York Philharmonic: 1999 as Associate Principal Cello
Teaching: Has a few private students
Music she listens to now when relaxing: Jazz

"When I was four years old, my mother gave me a little violin in a plastic see-through bag. I was curious about it, probably at first because it was in that see-through bag," says Hai-Ye Ni. Then her mom taught her how to play it. "I thought it was fun."

Hai-Ye's mom played cello in an orchestra in Shanghai, the city in China where they lived. Her mom had wanted Hai-Ye to play cello, but it was hard to find child-size cellos in China back then. Right before Hai-Ye was born, times had been tough in China, especially for musicians. The government had said musicians could play only Chinese music, not music written by foreigners like Ludwig van Beethoven and Johann Sebastian Bach. But by 1976, when Hai-Ye started violin, things were a little better. Musicians could play Beethoven and Bach again without getting in trouble, although it was still hard to find their music. Her mom had to borrow music by Bach from a library or from friends, and sometimes she had to copy it out by hand.

Hai-Ye's mom was also a cello teacher. "We lived in a tiny room: my mom, my grandmother, and me. My father had to work in a different city. I would sit on my bed with my toys while students were there taking lessons. Sometimes my mom would tap out a rhythm for them. I would get it right away, but they didn't. She spent so much time with them that I would get jealous. I felt they were taking her away from me. Then they would give me a present, like a big doll for New Year's. So I loved them again. I liked the time I spent with my mom on violin, but I didn't like practicing. After a while, I was ready to try something new."

"IT FELT NATURAL TO SWITCH"

When Hai-Ye was seven, her father found someone who made a small cello just the right size for her. "It wasn't a very good instrument, but I liked it," she says. "I was glad to stop violin. I had been hearing cello for so long. I liked the sound of cello and that the instrument was bigger than violin. I liked practicing cello more than violin. Cello came easily. It felt natural to switch."

In two years, she became good enough on cello to go to a special school at the Shanghai Conservatory. Part of each day was regular school—the rest was music. "I had very good training. We had to practice two hours a day in school," she says. "They had a lady who walked around the practice rooms to make sure kids were in their rooms practicing, not talking." It was a tough school. Kids worked hard. There wasn't much time for fun. "There was a Ping-Pong table outside a classroom, and every chance I got I would play. But the school was fun in the sense that I liked performing."

"A HUGE CHANGE"

She had a chance to do some amazing performing when she was twelve. She was one of three students at her school chosen to perform in the United States for a month. "I was so excited," she says. She and her schoolmates gave concerts in five cities, including a performance at the White House.

While performing in California during that trip, Hai-Ye met someone who would change her life: a cello teacher from the San Francisco Conservatory. "Before I came to the U.S., the teacher heard a tape of me playing. She couldn't believe a kid could play that well. She came to hear me in person." The teacher was so impressed that she helped arrange for Hai-Ye to come to California the next year to study.

So when Hai-Ye was thirteen, she and her mom left China and moved to California. Her mom found work teaching cello. Her dad had managed to come to the U.S. also and was in California, working as a scientist in a laboratory. "It was a huge change," says Hai-Ye. "I spoke a little English, but not enough. The first semester in junior high I didn't do well. I failed all my classes because I just could not understand anything. I would stay up late looking up words in the dictionary. Then I began to do better."

"WHAT MUSIC WAS ALL ABOUT"

On Saturdays, she took cello lessons and other classes at the San Francisco Conservatory. "I had already learned the technique of playing cello in China. Technically, I was very good. I could play anything. But if you just play the notes, you don't really get to live it," she says. "It was only after I came to the U.S. that I really understood what music was all about. I learned about the culture and history behind the music." She was entering a new stage in her performing by learning how to bring her music to life. "I would try to imagine stories when I learned a piece. I tried to understand what a piece was about. My teacher would help. I would think about my own experiences that came close to what the music meant. I would listen to a recording of the whole piece I was learning, not just my part. How does my part fit in? When I was fourteen or fifteen, I also learned to practice slowly. As a young child, I was too impatient for that. I always wanted to play things fast."

She practiced several hours a day but still had time for fun. "I did a lot of swimming, and I loved volleyball." She also went to music camps in the summer in Maine and New York.

"When I was in high school in the U.S., I started doing music competitions," she says. "I would take two or three weeks off from school to do them. When I came back, I would be really behind. Homework took up so much time. I wanted to focus on music." So she quit high school after two years and enrolled in a college-level program at the San Francisco Conservatory.

CONCERT WATCH

Some musicians move around in their chairs while playing in a concert; others don't, thinking it might annoy other musicians or the audience. Often the leader of a section—the principal—moves to the beat to help others in the section play the same. The Philharmonic's principal cello, Carter Brey, likes to move. "My moving seems to help the section," he says. "To me, music is all about rhythm and moving. I can't *not* move." When Hai-Ye Ni fills in for him as principal, she says, "I try to move, too, but maybe not as much as he does."

THE PATH TO THE PHILHARMONIC

Two years later, at age eighteen, she won first prize in a big cello competition in New York. She was the youngest person ever to win that competition. It helped start her on a nine-year career of playing both as a guest soloist with orchestras around the world and as a cellist in chamber music groups. She kept entering more cello competitions and doing well in them. Along the way, she earned a college degree from the San Francisco Conservatory and a master's degree from the Juilliard School.

During her travels, she met the Philharmonic's Carter Brey. He told her the Philharmonic needed another cellist and suggested she try for the job. Like Carter, she was growing tired of all the traveling a soloist does. So she tried out and in 1999 won the job of being the Philharmonic's associate principal cello. "It's a great opportunity to play with the Philharmonic, to learn so much wonderful music," she says. Orchestra members play many more pieces than a soloist does. However, she still finds time to perform as a soloist now and then and to play chamber music, too.

She's a U.S. citizen now. Her parents still live in California. A few years ago, Hai-Ye went back to China for the first time to perform as a soloist. "For a long time we didn't go back to China because we weren't sure we would be allowed to return to the U.S. It took a lot of courage for my parents to move here so I could study music." Now things are better in China than when she was a girl.

Hai-Ye arrives for a rehearsal with her cello strapped to her back.

"I'm so glad to have had both: to grow up in China as a child and then come here. I feel my life is so much richer. Music is the most amazing thing in the world to me. It can move you. It can enlighten you. It makes you a better person. I can't imagine a world without music."

*Pascual Martinez Forteza played on some of the
best youth soccer teams on the Spanish island of
Mallorca where he grew up.*

PASCUAL MARTINEZ FORTEZA

Clarinet

Age when he started clarinet: 10
Favorite books as a kid: Comic books
Pet he had as a kid: Parakeet named Clarín
Other activities as a kid: Soccer, swimming, biking
Other activities now: Swimming, biking, staying in touch with friends in Spain on the Internet, watching soccer games
Grew up in: Palma (on the Spanish island of Mallorca)
Education: Barcelona Conservatory in Spain; University of Southern California
Before the Philharmonic: Cincinnati Symphony Orchestra
Joined New York Philharmonic: 2001
Teaches: Private students in New York and at a summer festival in Spain
Music he listens to now when relaxing: Opera, Spanish pop music, Latin, jazz

"I started playing soccer when I was eight years old," says Pascual Martinez Forteza. "I played on some of the best teams in my city. We won a couple of championships. I was the goalie. Sometimes when I blocked a goal, I saved the whole game. It was fun." Being on a championship soccer team is a big deal. It's an especially big deal in Spain, where Pascual lived. Soccer is the most popular sport there. He grew up on Mallorca, an island in the Mediterranean Sea, just off the eastern coast of Spain.

"Sometimes I had injuries on my fingers when the ball hit them," he says. That was a problem

INSIDE SCOOP: CLARINET

<u>GOOD POINTS:</u> "It's not too hard to make a sound on clarinet when you start," says Pascual Martinez Forteza. A clarinet is also small and easy to carry around. Like every musician in this book, he thinks the sound of his instrument is the best.

<u>BAD POINTS:</u> "At first it's hard to learn how to blow into the mouthpiece with enough pressure to make the reed vibrate," he adds. "In the beginning you squeak a lot. Squeaks come from the reed if you're not using the right pressure with your lips or if you blow too hard. If the reed gets chipped, it won't vibrate. You have to take good care of the reeds. Some clarinet players make reeds. I buy them ready-made." Clarinet reeds are less expensive than oboe or bassoon reeds.

for something else he used his fingers for: playing clarinet. "My father plays clarinet. I heard clarinet ever since I was born," says Pascual. "My father had a clarinet waiting for me when I was big enough to reach the keys with my fingers. I liked clarinet and wanted to try." At age ten, Pascual started taking lessons from his father.

"My father liked soccer, too, but every time I hurt my fingers in a game, he said, 'Be careful.'" He didn't want broken fingers to stop Pascual from playing clarinet. Injured fingers weren't the only hassle. "The team trained three times a week. We played games on Saturday and Sunday, sometimes traveling to other parts of the island." Pascual also had lots of other things to do: school, homework, clarinet lessons, practicing, as well as music theory and singing classes at a conservatory. "Every day I was completely busy. I had no free time," he says. He felt he had to make a choice: soccer or music.

"KIND OF LONELY"

It wasn't just a love of the game that made Pascual like soccer. "With soccer you're with other kids on a team," he says. "Music was kind of lonely at first." At that time, schools in his part of Spain didn't have orchestras. Kids had to take music lessons outside of school, usually at a conservatory after school or on Saturdays. Pascual took clarinet lessons from his father, first at home and later at the conservatory where his father worked. But that conservatory didn't have a kids' orchestra either. Pascual didn't have much chance to make music with other people, except in the summertime, when his family spent a month each year in another part of Spain. They were visiting Pascual's grandfather, who also played clarinet. In his grandfather's town, there was a band just for woodwind instruments that Pascual's grandfather and father played in each summer. So did Pascual, starting at age ten.

Pascual's father taught him well. "He played in the lessons with me, and I tried to match his sound," says Pascual. "I'm sure he was harder on me than on other students. I *had* to practice every day because he was at home and heard if I didn't. But when you're ten or eleven, sometimes you don't want to practice. You want to go out with friends. I think when you're ten or eleven you don't need to practice too long. My father wanted me to practice an hour or two each day. Now I see it was good he made me practice. It became a habit. Now I like to practice. But back then, it was boring at times." He was glad to blow off steam with soccer. "Sports are important for kids to do, to develop their bodies. When you're a kid, it's important to learn to do many things, not just music, and not just sports."

"SOMETHING I COULD REALLY LIKE"

"When I was sixteen, I realized that I was not good enough at soccer to be a professional goalkeeper and so I decided to go for music," says Pascual. He was more interested in music by then because of a new professional orchestra that had started up the year before on Mallorca. Up until then, Mallorca had only an amateur orchestra that was pretty good, but not great. With the new professional orchestra, terrific young musicians traveled to Mallorca to play. Luckily, Pascual's father was good enough to be in the orchestra, too, and Pascual began hanging out at rehearsals.

"Wow," remembers Pascual, "the new orchestra sounded so much better. I fell in love with the music they played. I thought, 'This is something I could really like.' I became friends with the musicians. I began to practice clarinet a lot more. After quitting soccer, I had

---

PRACTICE TIP

IMAGINE: "When I was a kid, I put words to music I was learning," says Pascual Martinez Forteza. "It's fun. Kids learn songs so fast. If you make up words to go with a melody, you can learn it faster." The words can be silly or serious, your choice. He also made up stories, as if the music were the soundtrack for a movie. "There are some parts of a piece that might even feel like a certain color to you, or a flavor." Trumpeter Phil Smith notes, "You want to have some kind of a picture in your mind so you can tell a story with the piece." But he adds, "Creating your own image is what you do when you learn the piece. When you perform it, that image is underneath your playing. It's part of you, without your actually having to think about it directly while you perform." Not all musicians in this book use this approach, but several do and find that it helps.

Pascual shows off his clarinet at a workshop for teens.

more time to practice. From ages sixteen to eighteen, I really concentrated on music."

He had found ways to make practice fun. "I liked to invent stories to go with the music," he says. He also began listening to the many recordings his father had. "My favorite was Mozart's Clarinet Concerto. It's beautiful. It's the best piece for clarinet. I started learning to play it." All that practicing paid off. By the age of eighteen, he was good enough to try out for Mallorca's orchestra when it needed another clarinetist. He won the job.

THE PATH TO THE PHILHARMONIC

Even though he had a job in Mallorca's orchestra, he knew there was more to learn. He enrolled at a conservatory in Barcelona, on the Spanish mainland. "It was hard because I was in the orchestra and had to fly to

CONCERT WATCH

You might see a clarinetist pull a cloth through the clarinet. That's done to wipe up spit that has collected in the clarinet. Some clarinetists might also change their reed if the old one isn't working well. "I always have extra reeds," says Pascual Martinez Forteza. You can tell when clarinetists and other woodwind players are about to change reeds: They start sucking on a little piece of wood, the new reed. Reeds have to be wet to work.

Barcelona every two weeks for classes." After graduating, he quit the orchestra to study in the U.S. at the University of Southern California.

"My idea was to spend two years in California, improve, and then come back to Spain," he says. But in the U.S. great opportunities opened up for him that he couldn't turn down. First, he won a clarinet job with the Cincinnati Symphony Orchestra in Ohio. A few years later, he tried out for the New York Philharmonic, an orchestra he used to watch on TV as a kid. "I never expected to get the Philharmonic job." But he did, in 2001.

He goes home to Spain each summer, sometimes playing in the summertime woodwind band he was in as a kid with his grandfather. A few years ago, his old orchestra in Mallorca invited him to be a guest soloist. He played Mozart's Clarinet Concerto, the piece he began learning as a student. "That was such a thrill," he recalls, "to be home and play that piece."

Pascual still does something else he started doing as a kid. He imagines stories to go with music he's learning. "We can't use words in a concert, but through music we can try to make people feel things. I always try to express something through music, and not just play the notes."

Hae-Young Ham sings on a TV show in South Korea.

HAE-YOUNG HAM
Violin

Age when she started violin: 11 (started piano at 7)
Pets she had as a kid: Dogs
Favorite books as a kid: Korean fairy tales
Other activities as a kid: Running, tennis, ice skating, Ping-Pong
Other activities now: Running, working out at a gym, playing with her kids
Grew up in: Seoul, South Korea, and Westfield, New Jersey
Education: The Juilliard School
Joined New York Philharmonic: 1986
Music she listens to now when relaxing: Jazz and opera

"I sang in a children's choir when I was four years old," says Hae-Young Ham, who was living in South Korea then. "We sang Korean folk songs on the radio. We rehearsed three or four times a week. It was like preschool. We sang well, and I loved singing. When I was about seven, I was in another children's choir that sang on television."

Hae-Young's interest in singing came from her mother. "My mom loved music and would sing to me all the time. She taught herself to play piano." Her mom thought that since Hae-Young

was doing so well with singing she might enjoy playing piano, too. So she started piano lessons when she
was seven.

"I didn't like piano," says Hae-Young. "I didn't
have such a good teacher. She was very strict. She hit
my fingers with a ruler if I made mistakes." No wonder
Hae-Young didn't like to practice. Piano clearly was
not working out for her. Maybe there was another
instrument she would like more. An older cousin
played violin and knew a violin teacher who was good
with kids. He suggested Hae-Young try studying violin with this teacher. So Hae-Young switched instruments and at age eleven had her first violin lesson with
this new teacher.

"I loved the violin," says Hae-Young. "The sound
was closer to the sound of the human voice than piano.
Playing violin seemed like singing. I also liked feeling
the strings and using the bow." She liked the teacher,
too. "He was much more supportive. Having an
encouraging teacher is so important."

"MORE CHALLENGING"

"Age eleven is late to start violin," says Hae-Young.
"But I already knew how to read music from singing
and piano. Singing also helped because it teaches you
how to express yourself musically. Violin is such an
expressive instrument. I advanced pretty quickly." She
didn't mind that it was hard at first to play in tune on
a violin. "That just made it more challenging than

piano. Maybe that's why I liked violin. I also liked that you can play in an orchestra with violin. When I was about twelve, my mom took me to hear a concert of a famous Korean woman violinist playing with an orchestra. I thought, 'Oh, I want to be like her.' I thought being part of a big orchestra looked so great." Soon, Hae-Young found out just how much fun it was; she started playing with a Korean youth orchestra.

"I also liked sports," she says. "I was a good runner and loved playing Ping-Pong. I played tennis in the summer and skated in the winter. I loved being outdoors. Sometimes it's frustrating to be cooped up in a room practicing violin. When I felt frustrated, I'd go outdoors and run, or I'd play Ping-Pong. I'd get refreshed and then come back to practicing."

"BIG SACRIFICE"

She started entering violin competitions—and winning them, too. When she was fifteen, a violinist who had studied in the U.S. heard Hae-Young play. This violinist thought Hae-Young was so talented she should go to the U.S. to study in a program for kids at the Juilliard School, its pre-college program. Hae-Young's parents thought this was a possibility too good to pass up. So the whole family moved to the U.S. the summer Hae-Young was fifteen.

However, she hadn't been accepted into Juilliard's pre-college program yet! In fact, she hadn't even

PRACTICE TIP

DIFFERENT RHYTHMS: "When I practice, I take a section I'm having difficulty with and work on it over and over. I play very slowly," says Hae-Young Ham. "Sometimes I practice the section in a different rhythm than the one that's written on the page. That helps you learn the notes." It's amazing but true. If you take a string of tricky notes that are driving you crazy and challenge yourself to play them in lots of different rhythms, that actually helps your fingers get used to playing those notes. One time you might play them in a jazzy rhythm, or you might try a hip-hop rhythm. Many musicians do this. It's like a game, a way to make your brain wake up and pay attention to what those notes are. Of course, messing around with rhythm is only for practicing. After using this trick to master a pesky series of notes, Hae-Young goes back to practicing them in the correct rhythm.

applied to the school. The tryout wasn't until the fall. The family was taking a big chance coming to America.

Hae-Young's family settled in a New Jersey town, not far from New York City. Her father found a job. Hae-Young headed off to music camp in upstate New York to get ready for her pre-college Juilliard audition. "I liked practicing by then," she says. "I also had this sense that my parents had made a big sacrifice and I really needed to do well. But it was hard because I spoke maybe ten words of English."

"HIGHLIGHT OF THE WEEK"

One of the teachers at the camp was also a teacher at Juilliard. Over the summer, that teacher really came to like Hae-Young's playing. That made Hae-Young feel more confident when it was time to audition. She played well at the audition and was accepted into the pre-college part of Juilliard, a program of music classes on Saturdays for kids who haven't finished high school.

During the week, Hae-Young went to regular high school in New Jersey and did pretty well. "I loved math," she says. "I couldn't do sports because after school I was so busy practicing violin."

On Saturdays, she took a bus by herself into New York City to go to Juilliard. "That was the highlight of the week," she says. "It was great being with other kids who shared the love of music." She took violin lessons and other music classes there and played in the pre-college program's orchestras.

In her last year in high school, at age eighteen, she won a competition that had as its prize a chance to play in a concert with the New York Philharmonic.

Hae-Young and her daughter make music together.

THE PATH TO THE PHILHARMONIC

Hae-Young stayed on at Juilliard after high school, doing four years of college there and then two more years to earn a master's degree. She also played now and then with various orchestras, including one in Florida. In 1986, she signed up to do another program at Juilliard. Then a violin position opened up at the New York Philharmonic. "I went for the audition because I thought it would be a good experience, to help me get ready for other auditions. I never thought I would get

CONCERT WATCH

An orchestra's violinists share music stands—not to save space, but because the music usually comes on several pages. To turn a page, a violinist has to stop playing for a few seconds. If all violinists did that at once, there would be a big hole in the sound. So there are two violinists to a stand, with both of them playing the same notes. One turns the page while the other keeps playing. Usually the one on the inside (farthest from the audience) turns the page. The same is true of other string players. Strings play almost all the time in symphonies. It's important to keep the sound going. Woodwind and brass players don't play as constantly. Often their page turns can be arranged to happen when they're not playing. Most of the time, woodwind and brass musicians don't share stands because each of them usually plays different notes from others in their sections.

the job," she says. "I couldn't believe it when a man phoned me from the Philharmonic to tell me that I won the job. I actually screamed on the phone. I decided to leave Juilliard and join the Philharmonic. I feel so lucky. It's a thrill playing with the Philharmonic. I love going to work every day."

She has become a U.S. citizen, and her parents still live in the United States. She has been back to South Korea a few times, once with the Philharmonic when it went on tour there. "That was wonderful," she says. "I have friends and relatives there."

She still makes a habit of practicing violin every day. "Being a musician, you become an amazingly disciplined person," she says. "Practicing becomes part of your life, like brushing your teeth. You don't skip. You just do it." She has also started practicing another instrument: piano. Her young daughter plays piano in a program in which parents are supposed to play along with the kids. "I practice with her every day," she says. "My musical life has come full circle. Violin is my profession, but now I'm returning to my childhood experiences. I'm not only playing piano, but I'm also singing with my daughter. I love piano now!"

As a young boy, Jon Deak begged his parents for a piano.

Jon Deak
Bass

Age when he started bass: 15 (started piano at 5)
Pets he had as a kid: Cats named Rosie, Sammy, and Grunky Bunkle
Pet he has now: Dog named Lieah
Favorite books as a kid: *Call of the Wild* and other books by Jack London; science fiction
Other activities as a kid: Baseball, wrestling, golf, exploring outdoors, drawing
Other activities now: Mountain climbing, playing baseball, writing music, spending time with his children
Grew up in: Ogden Dunes, Indiana, and Oak Park, Illinois
Education: Oberlin College; the Juilliard School; Conservatory of Santa Cecilia in Italy; University of Illinois
Before the Philharmonic: Interlochen Arts Academy (teacher); Little Symphony of Chicago; American Symphony
Joined New York Philharmonic: 1969 as part of the bass section, and later became Associate Principal Bass
Teaches at: Elementary schools in New York and other cities where he gives music composition workshops for kids
While relaxing: He likes all kinds but prefers not to listen to music while relaxing so he can think up his own tunes

"I begged my parents for a piano when I was about five," says Jon Deak. "I loved to dance to classical music. I heard it on recordings and on the radio. I

INSIDE SCOOP: BASS

GOOD POINTS: "Bass has a wonderful, warm sound," says Jon Deak. "It can play so many different kinds of music and has a different name depending on the music. In bluegrass, it's called a bass fiddle. In jazz, it's an upright bass. In classical music, it's called double bass or contrabass. They're all the same instrument."

BAD POINTS: "It's huge." His bass is just over six and a half feet tall. There are smaller ones for young kids. As with cello, traveling with a bass is tricky. "It's also hard at the beginning to press the strings." They're very thick. Another drawback: There aren't many big solos for bass in symphonies. So Jon writes his own symphonies with terrific bass solos. He also takes pieces written for other instruments and adapts them for bass.

---

listened to Spike Jones on the radio, too." Spike Jones was a wacky performer who wrote funny takeoffs on pop songs. His band played instruments as well as noisemakers such as spoons, bicycle bells, whoopee cushions, and even guns. Jon loved it.

Jon knew nothing about piano other than that it had a lot of keys. "I figured you could play the most notes on it." His parents were artists, not musicians, and didn't have much money. But they found an old piano to buy. Jon began taking lessons from a teacher who lived near their Indiana home.

"She was an excellent teacher. I worked hard but was never a really good pianist," he says. What he liked most about the lessons was making changes in the tunes he played. "I changed a note here and there, or played the tunes on different parts of the piano. I wrote down the changes on the music. The teacher was very encouraging." Jon didn't realize it, but he was taking his first steps toward becoming a composer.

However, his piano and composing careers came to a crashing halt in middle school. His family moved to a town near Chicago, Illinois. He had a new piano teacher there. "She was *not* very encouraging," Jon says. She didn't like him writing new parts for his pieces. She wanted him to play them exactly as they were written. "So I stopped piano. I stopped composing. I dropped it like a hot potato. I was a little rebel."

"BEYOND THE NEXT HILL"

"In middle school I decided I wanted to become a base-ball player," says Jon. "I did pretty well. I could field almost any ball. I could hit a curveball, but my hitting average was only fair." He was on the golf and wrestling teams, too. He also loved exploring and having adven-tures outdoors. That had started back in Indiana when he lived near big sand dunes along the southern shore of Lake Michigan. "There weren't many houses around— just sea, shore, and sand," he says. "There weren't any trails. A buddy and I would explore to see what was beyond the next hill. Once we found a pond that wasn't on any map."

Then, during high school, his plans changed. He realized he wasn't good enough at baseball to go pro.

He began thinking about music again. His parents had taken him to a Chicago Symphony Orchestra concert, and he was thrilled. On his own, he began doodling around on his old piano at home. He asked his high school's orchestra conductor if there was an instrument he could learn. The conductor needed kids to play bass—the biggest, lowest-sounding string instrument. You stand up to play it or sit on a high stool. It has thick strings that you slide a bow across or pluck firmly with your fingers.

"I played a note on the bass and the physical vibration of it was really fun," says Jon. He also liked that the bass was kind of unusual, with not many kids playing it. That appealed to his sense of adventure, his love of exploring new things. So, at age fifteen, Jon began playing bass.

"STRONG PEOPLE PLAY MUSIC"

He took lessons from a professional bass player who was good at both jazz and classical music. "I practiced like crazy," he says. "I couldn't keep up with sports anymore. I kept jamming my fingers in wrestling. I kind of used that as an excuse to quit the team." He left the baseball and golf teams, too. His

---

PRACTICE TIP

KEEP GOING: "When you practice, you should be loving it," says Jon Deak. "Play pieces you like and have an idea of what you want to sound like. Then be patient. It's not going to sound the way you want right away. Kids get discouraged with music sometimes. But kids forgive themselves if they don't hit a home run right away. You see a baseball player hit the ball, and you get a clear image in your mind of what you want to do. Then you work at it until you can make a hit. That can take a while. It should be the same with music. Get a clear image in your mind of how you want to sound, a sound you love, and then work at it."

wrestling coach gave him a hard time about dropping sports. "I told him a lot of strong people play music. I was ready to devote myself full force to music."

He played in his high school jazz band and orchestra, and he tried out for youth orchestras and all-state groups. He was nervous at tryouts. To help him learn how to calm the jitters, his teacher suggested he do as many tryouts and performances as he could. "The first five or so you're going to mess up," Jon says. "So I entered every little contest. I fell flat on my face a few times." Gradually he learned how to tame the jitters. He managed to win a place in the Chicago Youth Orchestra, becoming its principal bass. He began taking lessons with a new teacher, a bassist in the Chicago Symphony Orchestra.

He also started composing music again. He wrote short pieces to play with friends, sometimes even in competitions. "In one competition a judge said, 'What's that piece you're playing? Who's the composer?' I said, 'It's me.' He said we couldn't play my piece. But the other judges said, 'Of course they can.'"

THE PATH TO THE PHILHARMONIC

Jon spent two years at Oberlin College in Ohio, and then he switched to Juilliard. After graduating, he taught high school kids at an arts academy. Then he won a special scholarship to study bass and composing at a music school in Italy for a year. Next, he studied at the University of Illinois. After that, he began trying

CONCERT WATCH

What does Jon Deak do with his bow when he's plucking the strings instead of bowing them? He clutches the bow with his pinky and ring fingers. Then he plucks the strings with his pointer finger or middle finger, and sometimes with his thumb, too. If he's playing a piece in which he's mainly plucking, not bowing, he attaches a pouch (a quiver) to the bottom of the bass and slips the bow in there when he's not using it. What about the endpin? "We're like cellists and stick our endpins into the floor," he says. If he plays in a hall where he can't do that, "I put a rubber tip on the endpin so it doesn't slide. However, a rubber tip dampens the sound a bit."

out for orchestras. In 1969, he won a place in the bass section of the New York Philharmonic, and later he became its associate principal bass.

Joining the Philharmonic was especially exciting because as a boy he loved watching the Philharmonic's Young People's Concerts on TV. The conductor who taught kids to love music on those TV shows was Leonard Bernstein. He was still with the Philharmonic for a few years after Jon arrived. "He was my hero," Jon says. Bernstein was a great example of someone who did it all: He played an instrument (piano) and was also a composer, conductor, and teacher. That inspired Jon to keep composing while playing bass in the Philharmonic. Jon's pieces have been performed by many orchestras, including the Philharmonic. "Some of my compositions have a little Spike Jones in them," he says, "and a little Beethoven, Stravinsky, and other composers, too."

Jon—and his bass—with a student at one of his Very Young Composers workshops.

Jon is also an enthusiastic teacher who encourages elementary school students to write music. He has taught workshops in elementary schools in New York City and Colorado. In his Very Young Composers workshops, he gives kids a chance to create their own music. Jon writes down the notes neatly so musicians can read them, but the notes all come from the kids. Then he brings in professional musicians (including some from the Philharmonic) to play the students' pieces. He says, "It's incredible the creative ideas kids have."

Harriet Wingreen liked to play dress-up as a girl.

Harriet Wingreen
Piano

Age when she started piano: 7

Pets she had as a kid: Cats, including one named Rusty

Favorite books as a kid: Books about children in other countries, books by Mark Twain, and Sherlock Holmes mysteries

Other activities as a kid: Collecting costumes and dolls from around the world, caring for stray cats, bike riding, roller skating, being in plays

Other activities now: Seeing plays and concerts, doing cryptic crosswords, writing a mystery

Grew up in: Howard Beach, New York

Education: Philadelphia Conservatory of Music; the Juilliard School

Before the Philharmonic: Chamber musician, accompanist, member of orchestras making soundtracks for movies and TV

Joined the Philharmonic: 1965 as a rehearsal pianist; 1983 as a pianist in concerts

While relaxing: "When I listen to music, I want to be totally listening, not doing something else at the same time."

"A piano came flying through the window of our apartment when I was a very little girl," says Harriet

INSIDE SCOOP: PIANO

GOOD POINTS: "You don't have to worry about making a sound as a beginner. The keys are all laid out before you. If you press a key, you make a sound," says Harriet Wingreen. Becoming familiar with the positions of the keys can help in learning to read music; the keys are arranged in much the same way that music is written on a page. Many who play other instruments find it helpful to play piano, too.

BAD POINTS: "Some people say how lucky pianists are not to have to carry their instruments with them. But you never know what kind of shape a piano you're going to play will be in when you get to a concert hall," says Harriet. It's smart to get there early to try out the piano beforehand. Some people say it's a lonely instrument. "It doesn't have to be lonely," she adds. "I played with groups of kids at music school and in the school orchestra during high school."

Wingreen. A visitor from outer space? No, it was an old upright piano her grandmother had but didn't use. She was giving it to Harriet's music-loving family. Harriet's family lived in a small apartment upstairs from the shop where her father worked as a tailor. The stairs were too narrow for a piano. Workmen used ropes to lift the instrument so it could go through one of the apartment's windows.

"I loved classical music as a kid," says Harriet. "I heard it all day. My father had the radio on all the time, playing classical music as he worked in his shop. He had no musical training but loved music. I was excited when the piano came. I started banging away on it, thinking I was making beautiful music."

Soon she really was making beautiful music. When she was seven, she began taking piano lessons from a neighbor. "I liked to practice and play my little pieces," Harriet says. "I loved the sound of a piano." After several months, a family friend suggested Harriet take lessons at a music school in New York City. "We had no money for that," says Harriet. "My mother took me to the school anyway, to audition for the school's director. It was a long trip. We had to take a bus, an elevated train, a subway, and another bus." Harriet played so well at the audition that she won a scholarship to attend the school for free. From then until the end of high school, Harriet traveled to the city every Saturday for her lessons. "I had a terrific teacher there and made friends with a wonderful group of kids."

"ON DISPLAY"

Harriet liked practicing piano but not performing. "I had fun playing for myself and my father and mother, but I didn't enjoy playing for my parents' friends," she says. "It was as if I was being put on display." She also didn't like it when her elementary school gym teacher wanted her to play piano during gym class. Everyone in school knew Harriet was a piano whiz. "My playmates were proud that I could play piano," she says. The teacher thought it would be great if Harriet played lively tunes to go with gym activities. "I hated that because I wanted to do gym with the other kids," says Harriet. "One day I didn't show up for gym. The teacher was angry. My mother was on my side and went to school to explain. They worked it out. I got to do gym."

She also didn't like the recital her music school had when she was twelve. It was at a big concert hall. She had a bad case of the jitters. "I was so nervous I thought I was going to die," Harriet recalls. "That's when I decided I didn't want to be a soloist." She preferred performing with a group, such as playing in small chamber music groups at music school or in the school orchestra when she was in high school.

She had other interests besides music. She took care of the stray cats in her neighborhood. "They would come to me, and I would feed them," she says. "Or I'd bring home a kitten that was hanging around the grocery

PRACTICE TIP

FOOL AROUND: "Kids should have a chance to experiment a little with their instrument, just sit and doodle around," says Harriet Wingreen. "When I was a child, you were supposed to practice only the pieces you had for your lesson and that was it. I wasn't given a chance just to fool around on the piano. That was a mistake." Experimenting a little on your instrument helps you learn more about it and can also help if you decide to play jazz. In jazz, musicians improvise (make up solos on the spot). "I love jazz," says Harriet. "I regret that I can't improvise."

Harriet shares tips on how to be a good sight-reader at a workshop for young piano students at the music school she went to as a girl—the Third Street Music School Settlement.

store." She also liked to play games outside with her friends, or to be busy at home with her collection of dolls from around the world. The dolls were gifts from an aunt and uncle who traveled a lot. Her relatives also brought costumes that she used in playing dress-up.

By high school, her interest in dress-up had changed to an interest in theater. But being in a lot of high school plays caused a bit of a slowdown in her piano career.

"THE ZOMBIES"

"In high school, I wasn't practicing piano much anymore," says Harriet. "My piano teacher said, 'I don't care if you practice or not, but come for your lesson every week anyhow.' So I would go to the lesson and we would sight-read a lot of music, mostly new, mod-

Harriet helps a student relax a little during a sight-reading workshop.

ern pieces." (Sight-reading is playing a piece you've never seen before.) "I found this new music exciting and challenging. It was the best thing that could have happened to me. I could have quit piano. But my teacher kept my interest going." Harriet's aunt and uncle kept her interest going, too, by taking her to concerts in New York City. "I heard all the great pianists," Harriet says.

She did a lot of sight-reading with kids from the music school, too. "We formed a club called the Zombies. We would go to someone's apartment and sight-read all kinds of music. We'd make up our own musicals, with dancing. We had a wonderful time. We all became fantastic sight-readers."

"STARTED ME OVER"

After high school, Harriet realized that what she loved most was music. She won a scholarship to study with a teacher from the Philadelphia Conservatory of Music for two years. Then she got up the courage to audition at Juilliard. In one part of the audition, the judges gave her a piece to sight-read. She played it so well the judges thought she must have seen it before. They pulled out a harder piece. Harriet aced that one as well. They were very impressed with her sight-reading skills, accepted her into the school, and gave her a scholarship. But soon she found that sight-reading would take her only so far at Juilliard. She had some catching up to do.

CONCERT WATCH

Many orchestral pieces don't include a piano at all. In some pieces, an orchestra's pianist may play other instruments besides piano, such as a harpsichord, an early version of a piano with a quieter sound. Or the pianist may play a celesta, which looks like an upright piano but sounds like tinkling bells.

"I had wonderful teachers as a girl, but they didn't concentrate on technique," Harriet says. A Juilliard teacher fixed that. She had Harriet learn a better way of using her fingers on the keyboard. "She started me over, working on technique. For six months I did nothing but scales and arpeggios. She helped me learn to play more easily and produce a better sound."

THE PATH TO THE PHILHARMONIC

Her Juilliard teacher thought Harriet should become a soloist. But Harriet preferred playing in a group. For several years after Juilliard she was in a chamber music group. Then she was an accompanist, playing piano for choral singing groups, dance companies, and even for the famous clarinetist Benny Goodman when he played concerts of classical music. She also played in orchestras that recorded soundtracks for TV shows.

In 1965 she got her big break. The New York Philharmonic had a concert coming up in which eight singers would perform with the orchestra in a symphony by Gustav Mahler, his Eighth Symphony. Leonard Bernstein, the conductor, didn't want all the orchestra's musicians to have to play their parts over and over while he worked mainly with the singers. He asked Harriet to help him rehearse the singers. She would play a special version of the symphony in which the other instruments' notes are written down in such a way that a pianist can play them. She had only a day to get ready. Her skill as a sight-reader came in handy. She did so well she became the Philharmonic's regular pianist at rehearsals like that. In 1983, when the orchestra needed a new pianist to play in concerts, Philharmonic officials knew where to turn. They asked Harriet, their favorite rehearsal pianist, to take the job. "I don't get nervous when I play with the Philharmonic," she says.

Here are most of the musicians featured in this book, taking a break during a rehearsal.

BACK ROW (LEFT TO RIGHT):
Carter Brey, Jon Deak, Sherry Sylar, Joe Alessi, Judy LeClair

MIDDLE ROW (LEFT TO RIGHT):
Jerry Ashby, Pascual Martinez Forteza, Cynthia Phelps, Sheryl Staples, Hai-Ye Ni

FRONT ROW (LEFT TO RIGHT):
Chris Lamb, Mindy Kaufman, Phil Smith

(NOT SHOWN: *Harriet Wingreen and Hae-Young Ham*)

Musical Teamwork

The musicians you've met in this book followed different paths to reach the New York Philharmonic, but now they're all on the same team, making music together. It's a big team, with 106 musicians in the orchestra. It has a big season, lasting about ten months, much longer than a major league sports team's season. Each week, Philharmonic musicians have about four rehearsals and play in three or four performances. The orchestra gives about 180 concerts a year, more than the roughly 162 games major league baseball teams play in a regular season or the 80 or so games of an NBA basketball season. Like a sports team, Philharmonic musicians need to work well together. Here are some of their teamwork skills.

READY, SET, GO: "We have to learn our parts in a piece before the first rehearsal for a concert," says Sherry Sylar. That way the orchestra doesn't waste time in rehearsal with musicians trying to figure out which notes to play. "I get my part from the orchestra library several weeks before the first rehearsal and practice it on my own."

FOCUS: "You have to really concentrate in rehearsals and performances," says Pascual Martinez Forteza. "You might be tired or you had an argument with someone at home, but you have to walk onto the stage and forget everything else and just concentrate on the music."

PRINCIPALS FIRST: To save time and confusion in rehearsals, the conductor speaks mainly to the principal player if there's a problem with how his or her section sounds. Then the principal will talk briefly with musicians in the section to be sure they know how to change things. If members of a section are confused about something, usually they ask the principal instead of bothering the conductor. If the principal doesn't know the answer, he or she will ask the conductor.

NO STARING: When musicians have a solo or a tricky passage to play, other musicians don't turn and watch. "If you see someone turn around to look, it takes your concentration away and you think, 'Why did they turn around? Did they think I didn't play well?' So people tend not to do that," says Sherry.

CLAM UP: "We play so many notes in so many concerts that chances are at some point you're going to make a mistake in a concert," Sherry adds. Yes, even professional musicians make mistakes, or "clams," as trumpeters call them. Often it's a little mistake, such as playing a note slightly out of tune or a bit too loudly. However, musicians don't make a face to let the audience know. Everyone keeps on playing as if nothing happened. "You forgive yourself and keep going," says Cynthia Phelps. "The minute something happens, we say it's 'ancient history.' Don't think about it while you're playing or you'll make more mistakes. Later at night, when you're home in bed you can think about how it happened."

GET ALONG: "We work so closely together that there will be times when you're angry with somebody in the orchestra. It's like a big family," says Sherry. As in a family, people make room for others' moods and don't get hot and bothered by little things. "You make some good friends, especially with those who sit closest to you in the orchestra," adds Sherry. She gets together for dinner with her orchestra friends. Joe Alessi and others in the trombone section play golf with one another. Hae-Young Ham is friendly with those who have kids the same age as hers. "Their kids come to our birthday parties. My kids go to theirs."

GETTING DRESSED

Like a pro sports team, Philharmonic musicians wear a uniform. Some musicians put on their concert outfits before leaving home, but most come to the concert hall in regular clothes and change there. "We have big lockers where we keep our performance clothes," explains Hae-Young Ham. For evening concerts, men wear black tuxedos; women wear long black dresses with long sleeves, or long black skirts with long-sleeved black tops. For afternoon concerts, men wear white shirts, ties, and dark jackets and slacks; women wear long-sleeved black tops, but may wear black pants instead of skirts. "At New Year's Eve concerts we can wear colorful dresses," says Hae-Young. A woman may also wear colorful clothes if she plays a special solo, performing in front of the orchestra. That's why Cynthia Phelps isn't in a black dress in the photo on page 2. She was the special soloist that day.

TIME OUT: Each musician has some time off during the season. On her weeks off, Cynthia likes to perform as a guest soloist with other orchestras. She feels that the challenge of playing exciting solo pieces keeps her skills in top shape. She and others also play chamber music in their time off.

A NEW LOOK: There are some popular pieces orchestras play again and again. To keep that from becoming boring, Judy LeClair says that "it's important to bring something new and fresh to those pieces, to create new challenges for yourself." The conductor helps by guiding the orchestra to find new feelings and moods in a familiar piece. Pascual adds, "The orchestra can play a symphony ten times and it's never exactly the same. That's one of the things I like most about music. Each performance is slightly different. Music is like magic. With each performance you're part of something that's never going to happen again just that way. If you think that way, trying to find something new in each performance, you have fun every time, even with pieces you play again and again."

Glossary

ARPEGGIO Playing separately, one note after the other, a group of notes (three or four usually) that when played together make up a chord

BOW A stick with horsehair attached to it that a musician slides across the strings on a string instrument

CELESTA A small keyboard instrument that makes a tinkly, bell-like sound

CHAMBER MUSIC Music for small groups of musicians in which each musician has a separate part to play

COMPOSER   A person who writes music

CONCERTMASTER   The leader (principal) player of an orchestra's violin section, also the official leader of all musicians in the orchestra

CONDUCTOR   The person who stands in front of a group of musicians and directs them as they play

CONSERVATORY   A school of music

CORNET   A brass instrument that is similar to a trumpet, but with a more mellow tone

ENDPIN   A metal stick that comes out of the bottom end of a cello or bass

ÉTUDE   A piece of music designed to help a student practice technical skills (in French the word *étude* means "study")

IMPROVISE   Making up music (or anything else) on the spur of the moment

LONG TONES   A warm-up for wind and brass instruments that involves playing a note a long time

MEASURE   The small segment that a piece of written music is divided into

MELODY   The main tune of a piece of music

METRONOME   A machine that can be set to click out the beat at varying speeds

ORCHESTRA   A large group of musicians playing a variety of instruments

PITCH   How high or low in sound a note is

PRINCIPAL   The leading player of a section of the orchestra

QUIVER   A pouch attached to a bass to hold the bow

REED   A small piece of bamboo (or sometimes plastic) that fits

onto the mouthpiece of wind
instruments such as clarinets,
oboes, bassoons, and saxo-
phones

RHYTHM   The timing or beat of a group
of musical notes; the pattern
in time that they make

SCALE   A series of single notes that go
up (or down) in pitch
according to a certain pattern

SIGHT-READING   Reading the notes while
playing a piece of music
you've never seen or practiced
before

SOLO   A piece of music played by
one performer (the soloist),
sometimes with accompani-
ment

SYMPHONY   A large musical piece written
for an orchestra

TECHNIQUE   The ability to perform the
detailed skills needed to play
an instrument

TEMPO

The speed at which music is played

TONE

A musical sound; also the quality of the sound, such as whether it's mellow or brassy

TRANSPOSING

Changing the pitch of the notes in a piece without changing their rhythm or the relationship between the notes

TUNING UP

Making sure your instrument is "in tune" with all the other musicians' instruments so they play notes the same, not too high and not too low

Resources

About the New York Philharmonic

Founded in 1842, the New York Philharmonic is the oldest orchestra in the United States. Over the course of its long history, the Philharmonic has given more than fourteen thousand concerts. In addition to performing at Avery Fisher Hall in New York's Lincoln Center for the Performing Arts, the orchestra also gives free concerts in New York area parks and travels to present performances in other cities in the U.S. and around the globe. Every year, some of its concerts are broadcast on TV and radio and can be heard on the Internet, too, at the orchestra's Web site. The orchestra can also be heard on CDs that it records on its own recording label: New York Philharmonic Special Editions. For more information, contact the orchestra at:

New York Philharmonic
Avery Fisher Hall
10 Lincoln Center Plaza
New York, NY 10023
Telephone: 212-875-5900

Web sites:

www.newyorkphilharmonic.org—This is the main
Web site of the Philharmonic.

www.nyphilkids.org—This is the Philharmonic's
Web site just for kids.

ABOUT OTHER ORCHESTRAS

Here are two organizations that have Web sites where
you can find the names as well as Web site links for
hundreds of professional orchestras and youth orchestras in the U.S. and Canada:

The American Symphony Orchestra League

33 West 60th Street, 5th Floor

New York, NY 10023

Telephone: 212-262-5161

Web sites:

www.symphony.org—This is the main Web site of
the American Symphony Orchestra League,
where you can find out not only about other
orchestras but also about educational activities,
including Jon Deak's Very Young Composers
workshops.

www.MeetTheMusic.org—This Web site lists
upcoming orchestra concerts around the
country.

www.playmusic.org—This is the American
Symphony Orchestra League's Web site for
kids.

Orchestras Canada

56 The Esplanade, Suite 203

Toronto, ON M5E 1A7, Canada

Telephone: 416-366-8834

Web site:

www.oc.ca—This   is   the   main   Web   site   of
Orchestras Canada.

OTHER HELPFUL WEB SITES

www.menc.org—MENC: The National Association for
Music Education, an organization for music
teachers, has information on music education.

www.amc-music.com—The American Music Conference
has information on music education and also has
links to Web sites for other music organizations and
companies.

www.nationalguild.org—The National Guild of
Community Schools of the Arts lists names of
music schools around the country and has Web site
links to many of them.

www.vh1.com/partners/save_the_music/home.html—The
VH1 Save the Music Foundation is a nonprofit
organization dedicated to ensuring that "all
children have access to a quality education that
includes music." It sponsors musical instrument
donation drives and other activities.

www.fromthetop.org—The *From the Top* radio series features talented kid performers. You can learn more about them through this Web site.

www.mtna.org—The Music Teachers National Association Web site has a "Find a Music Teacher" feature that lists certified music teachers in each state.

FOR FURTHER READING

The Young Musician's Survival Guide: Tips from Teens and Pros by Amy Nathan (Oxford University Press, 2000). Tips for kids from professional musicians on how to practice and deal with other hassles involved in learning to play an instrument.

Marsalis on Music by Wynton Marsalis (Norton, 1995). Practice tips for young musicians from the famous trumpeter Wynton Marsalis, artistic director of Jazz at Lincoln Center.

Sound Choices: Guiding Your Child's Musical Experiences by Wilma Machover and Marienne Uszler (Oxford University Press, 1996). Helpful advice for families and their musical kids.

LISTENING GUIDE

Here are three well-known orchestral pieces that were popular with the musicians featured in this book when they were kids. You can find them at your local library or music store. These pieces demonstrate clearly for listeners the sounds of different instruments in an orchestra:

> A *Young Person's Guide to the Orchestra*,
>   Benjamin Britten;
> *Peter and the Wolf*, Sergei Prokofiev;
> *Carnival of the Animals*, Camille Saint-Saëns.

Other classical pieces mentioned in the book that were favorites of the featured musicians when they were kids:

> Concerto for Orchestra, Béla Bartók;
> Fifth Symphony, Ludwig van Beethoven;
> Clarinet Concerto, Wolfgang Amadeus Mozart;
> String Quintet in C Major, Franz Schubert;
> *Petrouchka*, Igor Stravinsky.

Acknowledgments

I'm very grateful to the fifteen New York Philharmonic musicians who are featured in this book for taking the time from their busy schedules to be interviewed and to share their childhood memories, along with precious childhood photos. Thanks also go to the following members of the Philharmonic's staff who helped set up those interviews, made available the orchestra's photo archives, and offered encouragement and support throughout this project: Kristen Houkom, Melissa A. E. Sanders, Bill Thomas, Meredyth D. Thomas, Pamela Walsh, and Theodore Wiprud, as well as former staff member Thomas Cabaniss. I'm also grateful to members of the musicians' families who shared their memories and photos as well: Mrs. Mary Brey, Mr. and Mrs. John Lamb, Mrs. R. M. LeClair, Mr. Derek Smith, and Mrs. Betty Staples. In addition, I'm so glad that Sheryl Staples's sister, Deborah, Mindy Kaufman's brother, David, and Cynthia Phelps's sisters, Melissa Beckstead, Sheila Johns, Shelley Johnson, and Stacy Wetzel, agreed to allow the book to show photos of themselves as children.

Special thanks go to the following educators who made possible many of the photos of musicians working with students that appear in the book: Iessa Mitchell, Musical Advancement Program, Juilliard; Barbara Field, Rosemary Caviglia, Mary Lou Francis, Third Street Music School Settlement; Michael C. Reingold, JCC Thurnauer School of Music of Tenafly, New Jersey; Bob Arthurs, Katie Coppinger, Dr. Aaron Flagg, Rose Matthews, Music Conservatory of Westchester; John Paul Lacovara, Curtis Institute of Music; Ralph Wittal, Richmond Hill High School; and David Walsh, Leonia Middle School. Thanks also go to the following students who appear in photos in the book: Alison Candusso, Edwin Christian, Michal Emanovsky, Chaneice Frails, Kelvin Garcia, Anne Kay, Alice Kim, Lila Low-Beinart, Cesar Manon, Memie and Miru Hwang Osuga, Chase Park, Aneat Salcedo, Iwon Sato, Anna and Yonatan Sherman, Eli Soto, Orly Tahalov, Mayumi Tateishi, Ariana Wong, and Alex Zhang.

I'm also grateful to the photographers whose work appears in the book: Susan Johann, Lisa Kohler, Christopher Lee, David Morris, Yeui Park, Leo Sorel— and particularly Michael DiVito, who took so many wonderful photos of musicians and kids specially for this book.

All quotes from musicians in the book come from interviews conducted by the author, except for the final quote by Philip Smith in the main text of his chapter; this quote appears in one of a series of Web interviews by Beth Nissen on the New York Philharmonic (http:// archives.cnn.com/2001/CAREER/trends/02/22/nyphil. trumpet/index.html).

Warm thanks also go to the following people for sharing their thoughts and providing encouragement in the long process of bringing this book to life: Eleanor Ball, Joanne Bauer, Theresa Chong, Judy Crawford, Hiroko Miyake Dutton, Michele Eaton, Stephanie Fuller, Li-Chen Hwang, Polly Kahn, Mary Lamia, Dr. Yeou-Cheng Ma, Mary Moss, Michelle Nover, Thomas Osuga, Peter Schickele, Margaret Senko, Elaine Shapiro, Dr. Carolee Stewart, Dr. Andrew Thomas, and my editor Reka Simonsen. I'm also very thankful for the support and encouragement of my family: my musician sons—Eric and Noah—who inspired me to write books on music for kids; and my husband, Carl, without whose constantly upbeat attitude, gentle editorial suggestions, and generous financial assistance this book would never have happened.

Index

Page references in *italic* refer to illustrations.